"A heartfelt, heart-filling book about loss, grief, and enduring love. Chuck Murphree's words will stay with me and inspire me to write my own letters to the people I cherish. Beautiful."
— Jennifer Niven, #1 New York Times bestselling author

"Chuck Murphree shares a strikingly honest window into his relationship with his beloved mother in her final months. We gain insights into his life and hers as he shares loving messages as her strength and grit are challenged by a painful and debilitating illness. Disarmingly open and transparent, Chuck offers heartfelt glimpses into the lives they have shared. We learn of what contributed to the strength, fight and wisdom as well as the tenderness and acceptance that defines them both and their relationship. Rarely do we gain entrance so completely into a man's struggle, strength, commitment, and love as he says goodbye for now to the parent that shaped, encouraged, and loved him dearly. This is a touching tribute to the mother he dearly loved and loves. Chuck's relationship with his beloved mother inspires and teaches us of the invaluable moments and experiences that define an honest, authentic, mutually encouraging, and deeply loving relationship between mother and son."
—Dr. Scott A. Ritchie, clinical and consulting psychologist

"A heartfelt meditation on life and death. Told through a series of letters in anticipation of his mother's death, Murphee explores the raw, overwhelming emotions that come along with preparing to let a loved one go , from helplessness to rage to utter sadness. But it's also a celebration of a mother's love, of life itself, a soliloquy complete with gorgeous imagery and stark detail. Anyone who's lost a loved one, or anticipating losing a loved one—in other words, all of us—will feel less alone with this honest collection. A sheer privilege to read."

—Sally Collins, author of *Muddled Cherries*

"Chuck gives us his heart in these pages. We are allowed inside to witness his most intense and his most tender emotions. Through the gift of his experience, we learn what it is to be brave enough to love fiercely through loss."

—Michelle Konkle, peer specialist and somatic practitioner

Letters to My Mother

by Chuck Murphree

For information, please contact:
Ten16 Press, an imprint of Orange Hat Publishing

www.orangehatpublishing.com
Wauwatosa, WI

Letters to My Mother

by Chuck Murphree

For information, please contact:
Ten16 Press, an imprint of Orange Hat Publishing

www.orangehatpublishing.com
Wauwatosa, WI

To my mother,
thank you for raising a resilient son.

To Karen,
your love is what I am most grateful for.

Poems by Elizabeth Johnson Murphree

The Wait...

At night the souls of the dead
congregate, after dark, hunkering,
alone, they eye heaven. It is a
blueprint of hope.

Vanished...

Sunset delight, morning sorrow, ecstasy
throughout the night, paradise weeps as the
pain of leaving runs deep. Morning lingers,
sunrays dance off the dew, my soul aches
without you.

Prologue

*M*y mother suffered from Multiple Myeloma for over two years. I watched her body change color and disappear right before my eyes. She became skin hanging from bones, but what never changed was her eyes and her determination. Her eyes always showed pain. All of her life. It came from a difficult life of hard work and displaced love. Her determination, according to her oncologist, kept her alive, and without it, she would have died long before she did.

On July 7, 2023, we sat in the Oncology office waiting to hear the results of the blood work. This is when my mom found out that the treatments were no longer working, and have not been since March. I asked the question, "How long?" My mom also wanted the truth. Two months was the prognosis. It was then that I started to write my mom letters. I sent every one of them to her, except for the few after she died, of course. In these letters, there is the raw, unfiltered truth about a son's agony with losing his mother. The pain screams out onto the page as I realize I am completely helpless. There was absolutely nothing I could do to save her and keep her with me. All I could do is tell her how much I love her and do so by sharing my thoughts about her death, her life, and what losing her means to me. These letters are my last words to her.

My mom told me before she died that these letters will help others understand their own pain with losing someone they love. "Share them," she said, "There are so many people grieving." I will try, Mom.

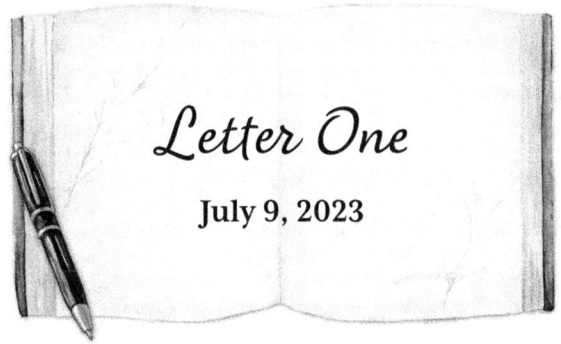

Letter One

July 9, 2023

Dear Mother,

So, we are here, that time we knew was coming. It's the great gig in the sky, the jumping-off point, where a new journey is at your doorstep. You will soon find out what is beyond this world, waiting, and you will get to see Charlotte again and tell her what you said, "I am home."

The doctor gave you two months. I don't look at life that way; maybe it's best to say that you gave your youngest son 637 months. I envy my siblings because they had more time with you, but time shouldn't be measured in minutes, or months, or years. Instead, the ticking clock should be measured in mindful breaths, moments that make you know you are alive, and I have had plenty of those.

As you know, I often write down my thoughts and feelings because conversations tend to get interrupted. The world doesn't seem to stop when a son has so much to say to his mother. Spoken sentences are often broken into fragments from nurses, doctors, and physical therapists. They are interrupted with everyday talk about the weather and things that no one can control, but still feel it's necessary to let their negative desires and false words fall from their swollen tongues, and you are often their sounding board. I understand because so am I. So, I do what I always have done when I need to get my thoughts out, uninterrupted, where I can say what is needed without competing egos and agendas hovering near and over me. This, I need to say because I am afraid that our time walking this earth together is narrowing.

It is the fifteenth round. I looked at you and said, "You have fought this thing for over two years. You have knocked the hell out of it the best you can, and it has knocked you down and you kept getting back up. A two-month prognosis doesn't mean you stop fighting; it's just a reality of our mortal lives." We are all impermanent and we all owe a death. One would think that with a comment like that I am unphased, accepting what is happening, and therefore my grieving will be short-lived. Grieving is perpetual. It's those same people that I have heard say throughout the past couple of years, "Well, she's eighty-four," as if putting a lengthy number on your age makes it okay or easier to lose you. I don't care if you were a hundred and eighty-four. There is never enough time, and when I hear these types of comments, I realize a few things: These people are possibly shallow. Perhaps, they are trying to console me in an inept way. Maybe they lost their parents, and with them, their empathy. Or, they just have no idea what to say and have never grieved for someone they hold dear to their heart. I refrain from telling them to go fuck themselves because I try not to let anger seep into my soul that often. I am afraid of the destruction it could cause. Look at me fighting as well, and you wonder where it comes from? The fifteenth round in life, those moments where all of your strength, determination, and resilience is something you have taught me to prepare for since I was a child. It has come in handy, especially the past few years.

I asked you recently, "What do you want? What do you need?" It is something that I would ask myself if I had a prognosis of two months. I wonder if you have things you want to say to others? Do you need to reconcile? Do you need to tell your kids how you feel about them and their lives, and perhaps give them more advice? Advice from a dying woman is something that should be heard with both ears. Maybe you have things to tell your grandkids, daughter-in-laws, and son-in-laws? Or, maybe you have said all that there can be in this lifetime and it's just time to be present and find joy?

You are still swinging, fighting this cancerous beast, and have said as much. You are determined to go home. To leave rehab and return to your dog and bed. To return to your painting and writing. You feel there are others who doubt you can do it, and I saw the gleam in your eye. I saw the feistiness and determination to say, "The hell with all that, I will show you I can do it." I even think you are determined to defy the two months you were given just to give one more punch to the heavy jaw of cancer. About going home you said, "I at least want to try." That word "try" is an important one. It is something that I see people not use. Instead, they don't try at all because of the fear of failure. The fear of not being able to do something. "Try!" Yes, fuck yes, go and try. I had a student ask me recently, "Why did you finish the Tough Mudder in a sling, with one arm, after they told you to go to the emergency room? Why do you do these grueling activities where you might not make it or get injured? Why do you climb mountains where there are animals that could eat you or you might get caught in a storm and die?" He wanted to know all of these things, so I told him because I needed to see if I could do it. I went on, "You need to challenge yourself and see if you have the grit necessary to do it." I have had people ask me similar questions about writing a novel. They wonder how I manage to write so much and find the time. I often reply, "You have to start and you have to try."

What happens when you don't try? Nothing! You taught me that. You helped develop the grit and resilience that I needed to say, "Nothing is going to keep me down. I'll die first." That has come in handy since I was a child, in the military, running races, walking to a mountain peak, and dealing with depression and anxiety. Many would read those words and say it sounds "Too macho" or "Too masculine." That's why I love being raised by a strong woman who taught her son that being masculine (That word that has become so negative because of false men modeling their insecurities) is okay. That being sensitive and empathetic and living a life helping others is also okay. You taught me not only to be strong and masculine but to be thoughtful and loving to my wife. I have sometimes said that I wish I had a male mentor growing up. There is truth to that, but I also recognize that I am one of the lucky ones because at least I had a mentor in you. Certainly, Dad taught me some things, mostly to be the opposite of who he was. Modeling for others happens in so many ways, negative or positive, and we all need to be reminded of that.

So, my dear mother, go and try like hell these next couple of months to live and die how you want to and never stop punching. I have never known you to quit. You have endured so much throughout your life, and yes, much of it has been tough. However, you are tough. I have told you to set aside any anger. Set aside any remorse or regret.

There is not any time for that, and I don't believe there ever has been. There is only time for being mindful, for finding joy, and even being grateful. As your son, I am grateful that I got to see you live eighty-four years. I am grateful that we have been given two more months because so many families do not get that time together. One has to find gratitude in times of distress and sadness. Gratitude allows us all to fully love one another and be present in the moments that we have left.

A couple of years ago, when you called me and told me about your diagnosis of Multiple Myeloma, I remember saying to myself, and probably to anyone that was near me if they were willing to listen, "Pay attention! Pay close attention to this woman who is about to teach us all another lesson." You have done that. You have taught us all that we must fight like hell for our lives. To never give up or give in and swing until the last bell is rung.

Love,
Chuck

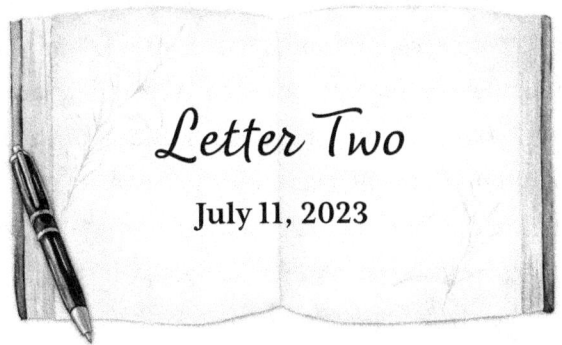

Letter Two

July 11, 2023

Dear Mom,

The anticipation of your suffering has tightened my throat. I can say I have been planning this for over two years, but I am still not sure what a world will be like without you, just a phone call away. One where I can't call you up and say, "Let's go for a ride," or take you to the bookstore. I am uncertain what that means, and I sit in tears, missing you already.

You have said often that death is a natural progression of life. This is true, I know. However, I think grieving is a natural progression of life as well. I have lost others, some tragically, and each death has changed me. It changed my eyes and how I carry my shoulders. The weight is heavy. I have become weary over the years, but also more mindful of the time I have left, whatever that may be, and living it to the fullest. Still, losing a mother, someone who gave you life, cared for you, and protected you from the monsters, is like losing an organ, a piece of my heart that lets life flow through it.

I have been randomly crying. It is something that needs to happen, and I do not attempt to stop it, for tears have a place on my cheekbones. They have a place on my shirt sleeve. I am doing what I have always done, modeling for other men that it is okay to express your feelings, your fears, and never steer away from the emotions that may pour out of you. Strong, confident men are able to sit with their feelings and accept any direction they may take them, and if that is weeping for the woman who raised you, who loved you with all of her heart, then let it happen as needed.

I recently came to see you, after we found out your time is now limited, from the woods where I find my breath. I walked the trail that day, some of it with my eyes closed, taking in the sounds of nature and walking each step by instinct. I am not sure why I closed my eyes to walk blindly, but I felt a need to navigate the trail by feel. Perhaps, it was to open all of my senses and become extremely aware of the life around and within me. Life! Oh life, that precious thing that so many waste or take for granted. So many forget why they are here or their purpose. More tragically, they never find that purpose and aimlessly drift. They scroll on their phones and social media for hours at a time and forget to live. Some will not like those statements. They will say that false messages on little screens are a good way to spend their time. To each their own, I suppose, but your looming death, like others I have witnessed, has made me hungry to live the life I want, my way, and be present. Yes, fully present, so I closed my eyes and walked a dirt path that led up and down and curved in and out between the towering trees. I could hear my heartbeat along with the trees swaying in the wind and the birds chirping. In the distance, I could hear the cranes and decided I am blessed. Yes, I am blessed with life. When I saw you after this hike, you said to me, "I wish I would have done that with my life. I wish I would have spent more time in the woods and on the trails, seeing the views and being around the animals. It's something I did all the time as a girl." Yes, I wish you would have too. It's healing. However, the stories that you told me about your adventures running through the Alabama hills inspired me to do what I do. It built a foundation. That's what parents should do for their children, build a foundation, a base, for us to build from. So many foundations are cracked.

I take the dead with me when I walk in the woods. Sometimes, I leave a piece of them on mountain tops. I know I will do the same with you. In fact, I have been taking you with me on my walks for a long time because I knew you would be at death's doorstep sooner rather than later. Death doesn't dismiss any of us. It wants our souls, and we all have to pay our dues.

I wonder, when will I pay my dues? Will you come for me, your youngest, and wrap your arms around me? When you do, will your face be without pain? Will you smile upon me and welcome me to wherever it is that you have been? If I am old, will you recognize my wrinkled face? I suppose you will, because my face is yours.

Love,

Chuck

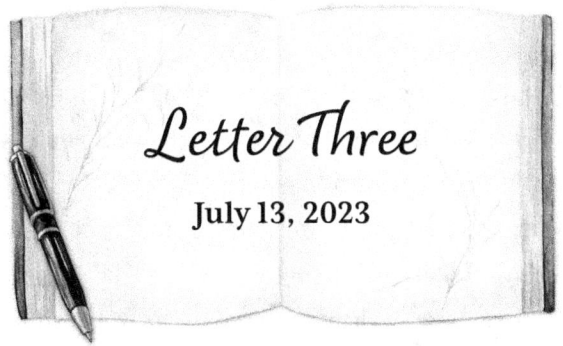

Letter Three

July 13, 2023

Dear Mom,

I woke up yesterday sitting on the patio in tears. It just hits sometimes. My heart hurts when I hear you pick up the phone knowing that in the near future I will not hear your Southern drawl say, "Hello, hon," and I won't get to say back to you, "Hey, lady."

It's the little things, isn't it? Mostly, it's just the conversations. The talks and telling stories will be what I miss most. I felt compelled to call you yesterday and tell you that I will miss you. As you know, I am a believer in telling people how I feel about them while they are here, with us. It's important that people know how we feel and how much we care about them.

So, what will I miss about you? Well, it goes back a lifetime, as far back as I can remember, which is about three years old. Dang, that's fifty years of memory with you. When you think of it that way, we have had a half-century together. We could grow two or three trees in that amount of time. I will most likely have another thirty or forty years walking this earth to miss you.

As a child, I miss opening up my lunch bag and finding a note that ends with, "Love, Mom." I miss being an eight-year-old boy watching Little House on the Prairie and laying against you, feeling the safety that a mother provides. I will miss drives in the country and trips to the bookstore. I will miss bringing you Egg Foo Young. I will miss receiving your text and written messages on my website after I spill my guts to the world trying to bring awareness about the darkness our minds can hold. And, I will miss our talks about that darkness, something we share, and the open discussions about depression and how we both put it into our writing. I will miss the taste of chicken and dumplings. No one rolls dumplings like you! I will miss telling our stories to one another and sharing what we have written. There are a million things I will miss, but as I said, it's the little things. It's sitting on your porch talking about life, past and present. It's hearing stories about your daddy and Uncle Curtis. It's picturing you as a girl running through the woods and skinning your knees and watching out for copperhead snakes. The thing I will miss most is your hugs and telling me you love me. To be loved, genuine love, is the greatest gift anyone can give. I ache at times because I know that you will not be here to tell me you love me. However, you have given me decades of all the love that you could provide, and it will fill my lifetime.

I will miss seeing your hands. They hold onto the history of our family. They have endured. They fed us. They sacrificed for us. Your hands have held all of us up.

I will miss how you have loved Karen. You have loved her like she was your own, and I appreciated that because she is a part of me. She makes me whole, and you knew that, so you took her in as if she were your daughter.

I am grieving. I have been for a couple of years. I have accepted long ago what the outcome would be, and now that we are here, my chest is heavy. It's as if the hand of God is pressing on my sternum and keeping the pressure there just enough for me to have to focus on taking a complete breath. However, as you know, grieving is natural and is going to happen. It is harmful to deny any feelings that may come to me, so I let them happen. I sit with them with a great deal of curiosity and offer myself empathy and compassion. I know that I will grieve for you for the remainder of my life, and that is okay. You were never meant to be here forever, but that does not make it easier. Still, it is why I have always prepared myself for suffering. We must learn how to suffer in order to have joy. It is something I have learned from Thich Nhat Hanh over the years. I am thankful I could share his wisdom with you.

I bring my grieving up because I want you to know I will be okay. I told Karen recently that losing you will hurt as if a limb is being taken from me, but I assured her I will be fine. I have to tell you this because you are my mother and have always worried about me. You have worried about some of the risks I have taken from running in mountain lion country, to mountain biking down steep grades, and climbing on tops of peaks. Mostly, you have worried about my depression and rightfully so. You know that I have sunken deep into the depths of my mind, the dark places where the monsters come to play. I have faced producing my own death, but I have survived.

I have become resilient and self-aware. I am okay and I will be okay after you leave. I am prepared for a long life. I do not deny the joy of living. I love life, and as I have said in my mental health talks, "Depression and anxiety are my superpowers." They have allowed me to understand myself and the world on a deeper level. I need you to know that I will be okay.

I will miss your eyes. They are mine. As I age, it is more and more obvious that I am my mother's son. Even through all of your pain, not just with the cancer, but all of your life, the blue in your eyes has never changed. The color remains true, watching over all of your children and their children, and they have always been determined. Your eyes tell another story, not unlike your hands, but they tell one of love and sacrifice, one of pain and agony, and of resilience and hope. Your eyes have seen a lot. They have been witnesses to enough happenings that it would fill several volumes of books.

What I will not miss is being your son. I am forever your son, your youngest child, one that dreams and walks in the woods, and one that decided long ago to live life on his own terms, which means I have faced many obstacles. When one chooses their own path and doesn't let others take it away from them, they are destined to face adversity. I am forever your son and will continue to tell my stories, our stories, because there are many to tell. I will finish the stories that you will not be able to.

Mom, I will miss you, but you have been making me ready for this day for most of my life. You have openly talked about death in such a way that I do not fear it. Your body will be free soon. It will go where you want it to, without pain, without remorse or sorrow, and you will be on a great journey. I will be on that journey too one day. I have too much to do for now, but someday I will see you again.

I have allowed myself to break a little during this time. I will put myself back together. I always do, but I need to crack a little to let the sorrow out. I was under anesthesia recently, and apparently, the nurse asked me if I had any pain, and my reply was, "Just in my soul." I don't think I said that without reason.

Mother, you will soon be a bird. Go fly and be free!

Love,

Chuck

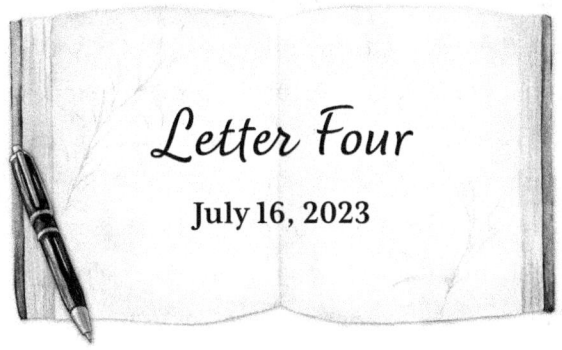

Letter Four

July 16, 2023

Dear Mom,

I hope I have become a good man. I didn't put a question mark behind that sentence because how else could you answer but, "yes." Still, I do sit and think about my worth, my growth, my purpose, and reason, and the life that I have paved for myself. Is it enough? Am I enough? I often reflect and ask myself, "Am I a good son? A good husband? A good friend? A good teacher? A good human?" I sit with these thoughts and wonder how I can improve. What else can I do to be worthy of the life that you gave me? Some would say this is too much pressure to place on oneself. However, I think we owe it to ourselves, to those that love us, and those who created us, to be the best that we can be and serve others. Am I serving others enough?

It is daunting sometimes to think, if lucky, that I only have thirty or forty years to do what I would like in order to accomplish what I will, which is to be there for others and have some impact. To be helpful. I have found that physically and emotionally, I must protect myself. I can only do so much, which is why I offer my written words.

They are for everyone and allow me to reach a wider audience. They allow me to help young people and older alike, to look within, and possibly help them navigate their darkness. At the very least, I hope my words are a comforting light to guide them a step at a time. My spoken words are for the people who come and see me, to hear my story, my truth, and understand that they are not alone. I also reserve the words that fall from my mouth to those that want to sit beside me, just a few of them because I would drain my reserves if there were more, and listen and offer what I can if they ask. Is this enough?

So, have I become a good man? Have I been a good son? I am becoming more confident, more encouraged that I am doing my best. I am trying to listen to my own words that I offer others. Many might look at these questions and think I am not confident or too hard on myself. The latter might be true at times, but not the confidence part. I feel that deep reflection can help map out the direction that we want to go in our life. Without asking these questions of myself, I am afraid I would settle, and to me, settling in life is not acceptable. I have never asked for riches or material items. They do not interest me. Most of what I do is for the love of a girl I met so long ago, but for me, I need little. I only want good food to nourish my body, peaceful trails to walk on, sunsets, the ability to travel, conversation that is meaningful, notepads to journal, books to read, and a place to explore with my thoughts and words, and love. That doesn't seem too much to ask. A man is always wealthy if he needs little.

Here is something I wish for you to recognize. As you go through the next few weeks, when your body starts to give itself away, little by little, to the death that will eventually come, I want you to know that your life has been worthy. You have talked to me in the past about things you wish you would have done, walking on the sharp edge of having regrets. As you know, I am not one for regret. I think your life has had meaning. From an early age, you have learned to endure and build resilience. That is something you taught me, and I am sure others. Your purpose was to raise a family, one that is often cracked and splintered, but you still raised us. As you see us gather with you, even the ones who are not there, whether living or dead, know that we would not be here without you, and their children and the children that will come later, would not be here either. None of us that has your blood flowing through them can deny that. If they are grateful for their life or their children's life, then they should be grateful to you. And there's more, as I watched you go through the hallways of the rehabilitation center, saying goodbye to the staff that has helped care for you the past month, they came to you, one by one, hugging you, and a few saying, "I love you." Your nurse cried. The impact you have on others is strong and will last. You have lived a life worthwhile. It has had purpose and meaning, and it is to be celebrated.

I had a dream the other night. I was floating on my back down a slow-moving river in between trees and mountains and I came to a rocky bank and you were standing there. You were not sick, not weary, but strong and able-bodied. I woke up after you reached your hand for me. Perhaps, I was dead in my dream or maybe, just maybe, I was more alive than ever.

Love,

Chuck

Letter Five

July 22, 2023

Dear Mom,

There is an agonizing anticipation to your death. Confusion and chaos are two words that come to mind. Yes, the chaos of death! The moments can feel completely overwhelming. Hell, it is more than overwhelming; it is a raging river, a flood, tornado, hurricane, and earthquake all wrapped up into one terrible storm.

One would like death to be peaceful. To simply go to sleep one night to a beautiful dream and have the hand of God come and reach for you, followed by a gentle, guiding light. I have not known death to work that way. Even our beloved Charlotte's death was chaos. The unknowing of why she was actually dying. "A stroke to the stomach," we were told. What the hell is that? There was not really a medical term, it seemed. Her blood pressure fell, and she died. As it happened thirteen years ago, it seemed like a donkey kicked my chest, right in the middle, above the rib cage, and took the wind from me. What led to her death was chaotic, unknowing, and the anticipation tore into all of us like a rabid animal. After she stopped breathing, we saw that light. All of us in the room did. I am not sure any of us knew what was happening, but something beyond us was there, and it took everyone to leave that space to recognize it fully and then hesitantly share what they saw later. The hesitance might have been from disbelief because it was the type of thing you read in scripture or see in the movies. All of us, even the skeptics, said that her death produced an immediate calmness to her face, making her years younger, and the pain, the turmoil that was in her mind and held in her face, went away. She was beautiful.

Still, what leads up to the actual death is not always beautiful. We need to be prepared for that. The world in general needs to be since it will happen to all of those we love. Death, I have found, wants to slap you in the face, cause a ruckus, and wake you up to your own life. Some of us listen, and some don't.

I had a glimpse of what is to come. For those that don't understand Multiple Myeloma (I didn't either), it is a slow, extremely painful, bastard of a disease. It takes to your bones and makes camp there, tormenting the spine with constant attacks of brutality. It's the type of pain that causes its victim to take oxy and morphine. The amount of morphine that a wounded soldier might take on the battlefield. That's what it is, a battle, a war, and it is ruthless with its arsenal. To win a battle, a war, chaos is a good strategy to confuse your enemy, and this particular cancer is a master strategist.

So, when I came to pick you up for your appointment, I found you in a different state. I will not begin to describe it, but as I have been witness to the chaos of death before, I thought it was starting, that final descent into the abyss. I figured we were at the doorstep. I sat across from you and tears filled your eyes, and I held your hand and gently kissed it, telling you how much I love you, and I told you I wanted you to have my strength, right then and there, I wanted you to have my strength. If I am anything, I am strong in body and mind.

We went through the motions that morning, finding out that the prognosis of two months may be a gift, and that a decline could happen at any time. This is what you and I have been talking about, and I have been trying to tell others. However, everyone needs to handle the process of dying and grieving their own way and at their own pace. I am far into this thing we call "grieving." I have rolled through it all and found my way to acceptance. Still, that does not make it easier. It just means that I am ready to stand with you and next to you while you enter this next journey.

We held each other yesterday, a mother and son, and I didn't want to let go, transferring you from the wheelchair to my truck, and you said, "I love you, son." Love is such an amazing emotion, feeling, and word. I was amazed that with all that you were going through in that moment, right then and there, that you thought of telling your youngest that you love him. That is what I will remember, your love.

You had a moment of clarity when we were driving and said to me, "Where are we going? Let's get out of here?" I am not sure if you remember this moment or not? It made me chuckle. It also made me become mischievous and I suddenly had this urge and said to you, "I have a full tank of gas. How about we just keep driving west until we come to some mountains?" I meant it at the time. You laughed at this and then replied, "I didn't think it would start happening so fast." And then we wept again. That is the chaos of death. Every emotion will come and go within moments of each other and swirl you around until you are dizzy.

The hospice nurse arrived shortly after we were home. The involuntary movements came back, you drifted in and out, and then told the nurse you were proud of me. She welled up in tears. I am unsure where that came from. You fell asleep shortly after and then woke back up in tears, looking at me and telling me that you are sorry. Yes, the chaos of it all. The emotions toying with your mind and body, but it is okay. It is all a part of what is happening and will happen. I sat there with the nurse talking. She asked about your family and I told her what I always say, "You find out a lot about people when there are stressful situations, especially death. You find out who they are." She agreed as she has been doing her job for a long time. I added, "They will all be here for her when they are ready. She is ready for them but they are not quite ready for her yet."

Hospice nurses were molded from the heavens. Being an empath, I can tell when I am in the presence of other empaths. The genuine ones. The people that can place themselves in your skin and walk around for a while. She was one of those. I love human connection. It is what we all need for survival. Though, I think our society sometimes forgets that. The nurse sat with my brother, who came to relieve me, and he and I talked about some of the realities that will start to happen. It is what is needed. I like to know what I am facing. She looked at me as I sat in tears holding your hand, "I can see your connection."

You slept and we planned. We started to plan for what appeared to be a more imminent death than we thought. I talked to my brother, he too is strong, and I am glad we are beside one another through this, and we talked about the reality that sat at our doorstep. We wept.

Then, I received a call later saying that you woke up and were your feisty, ornery, stubborn self. You woke up to your grandson hugging you and said, "Hey hon, how are you doing?" Your blood runs deep through him. You said you might have taken a little more morphine than you thought because your pain level was a six this morning. On a side note, when I told the nurse you said your pain level was a six, I said that means about an eighteen for the normal human. She laughed when I added, "She could handle medieval torture chambers if she had to."

So, the chaos of death came for a brief visit. It has us spinning. It was an adjustment to the new dose of morphine. Holy fuck! I still think about that sometimes. You have to take morphine for this pain. It makes me either break down or stand taller when I think about your pain. I either become the seven-year-old child that tries to hug the pain from your body and mind, or the fifty-three-year-old man who lifts you up, literally, and offers you his strength. We saw a glimpse of what would come. Maybe it was another lesson for us, to help us prepare and get our minds right?

Here is one thing, my dear mother. I have said that you are hard to kill. It is true. You do not lay down for anyone or anything. Hugh Glass has nothing on you.

I told the hospice nurse shortly after she arrived, after we developed a rapid rapport with one another, "I feel I have been baptized by her pain." She was curious about this. I told her I have experienced my fair share of pain in my life, both physical and mental. The physical has been self-induced through challenging my body and mind to see what I am capable of. The mental state is a lifetime of depression and almost a decade of anxiety and panic. I went on, "No one should ever compare their circumstances to another, for we all have our heartaches, and it can affect us in a variety of ways. There is no reason to compare pain, grief, depression, anxiety, or any emotion. Yet, I am humbled by what she is able to endure. It is something that makes me cry for her and feel proud. It's a strange feeling to be proud of your mother for how she handles her pain and dying. However, she is pure grit." The nurse listened intently to this and nodded for more, "We don't see this type of grit and determination often. Most people succumb to pain and their circumstances and roll over with their bellies in the air waiting to be taken by death or for someone to come along and save them." It's something I have come to be fascinated by. What makes people give up or fight?

I left the nurse that day and said to her as I looked over at you, "I hope you have time to get to know her. She is a remarkable person."

Mom, the day we had, I believe, has given us some insight into what is to come. The nurse, who has been a witness to souls fading from many, agreed. I want you to know that I am ready for the chaos of death. I will help you through it.

Love,

Chuck

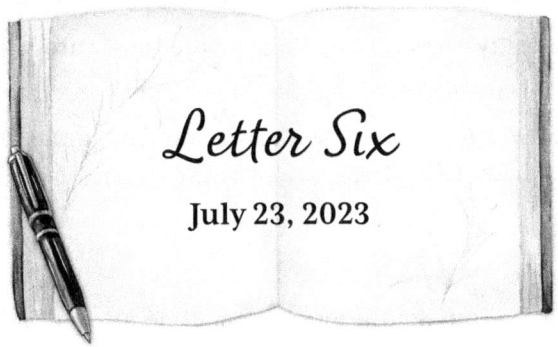

Letter Six

July 23, 2023

Dear Mom,

Three Sundays ago, I sat on my couch early in the morning, tears flowing hard like someone left the faucet running in the kitchen sink, two days after you were given the prognosis of two months to live. The thought came to my mind, "I wonder what foods she's craving?" It is strange when death is so near what thoughts may enter. So, I sent you a message and you replied immediately with, "Fried okra, black-eyed peas, greens, and cornbread." This didn't surprise me coming from a Southern girl. I immediately started to look for a caterer of soul food.

This is when I had this thought and ran it by you, "Let's have a celebration of life while you are here."

You replied, "Hon, I think that is a wonderful idea."

There are so many families that do not get to have a celebration of life while their loved one is still here, and we are fortunate to be able to. So, we scheduled it for one day after the thirteenth anniversary of Charlotte's death. For me, there was a sense of urgency to have the party. The reality of everything that you are going through and what is to come hit me like a wooden bat across the temple, and I knew it must be sooner rather than later. You are already starting to decline, lose your energy, and the pain and tiredness that comes with dying is creeping more and more into your skin and bones.

We feasted on Southern food, soul food, and added fried chicken and banana pudding to the list. As we sat under the shelter at Indian Lake, nature all around us, you were surrounded by family, immediate and extended, and I saw both joy and sadness simultaneously in your eyes. It occurred to me that not only are we, your children and grandchildren, all grieving, but so are you. How could you not be? You are grieving for all that you have lost and are losing. We spoke about this together. You are grieving for your loss of independence, your body failing, knowing that you cannot do all the things you want, and you are losing those you love around you. It's something that we do not often think about, that the dying are also grieving for their own death and the looming end that is so near. What a complete whirlwind of a mindfuck it must be to know that soon you will not be here. You will not get to taste food, watch movies, read books, write poetry, talk with friends and family, experience the sunset, and hug your kids. So, when the wind and rains came and the thunder clapped above us, I felt the need to scream out, "Behold!" with my hands held high in the air while the rain pelted down on me. I needed to lighten the mood, some of the natural tension that I knew would be present. You smiled and everyone else looked at me like I was crazy, especially when I ran out into the rain. What no one heard me say was, "Lord, you can't have her today." The storm was appropriate for this day of celebration.

Mom, you are tired. You have fought hard all your life, and now it is your turn to rest. You will find relief soon.

We celebrated you on Saturday, but I want you to know that I celebrate, and will continue to celebrate you, every day for the remainder of my life. When we stood and read your poetry, I mentioned that writing makes us immortal, and that if anyone ever wants to know what was on your mind, in your thoughts, they do not have to look much further than your writing. This is true of all writers, and as fellow writers, we locked eyes when I preached those words, not caring if anyone else heard them but you.

The days are coming to an end. As I stood with the hospice nurse yesterday, she told me that there will come a time when "The family" will need to take over care until longer-term arrangements are made. My chest became heavy, but it also raised a little higher knowing that I will be present to watch over you. Time will test us all, and time will eventually come for us too as our bodies, our life here, come to an end. Time is the great master. With each moment, every clicking second, we are all dying. The question I always ask, "Am I truly living?"

Love,

Chuck

Letter Seven

July 28, 2023

Dear Mom,

I recently stood in front of a crowd, with you next to my side, and proclaimed that when you told me about your diagnosis a couple of years ago, "I knew you would be teaching us a valuable lesson. If we pay attention, we are about to learn from you once again." I am learning from you as you face death. I am an attentive student, listening with eager ears and swallowing every word of every conversation that we have. We can learn a lot from the dying. Though I have learned so much from you throughout my life. The modeling and conversations and allowing your son to respectfully challenge your own thoughts and engage in meaningful dialogue. We don't talk about superficial things. It often goes deeper, but this only happens when we are alone. When there isn't the heaviness of entertaining a crowd.

Yesterday, we sat looking at your volumes of journals. You have told me for years that you wanted me to have all of your writing. This is important to me, as I hold your words, your experiences, your truth, and your pain close. I will admit, it took a lot not to break down when I knelt on the floor, you next to me in your wheelchair, and me holding it all in my hands. The words that hold your life. You said that many of your thoughts will be hard to hear, but as I have always said to you, "What do we have if not our truth?" I can handle your truth and I know there will be many experiences and thoughts that I may have to sit with for a while, and that is okay. I have no problem finding out more about my mother, even parts that may be difficult.

I started to think about what I carry that is yours.

I carry your eyes. The shape and size and the inquisitive look. Our eyes can show love and they can show anguish, and there are times when our eyes hold a similar glare. Our eyes see truth and filter out the bullshit that stands near. You have said I carry your Daddy's eyes, along with his temperament, which is being patient until there is no choice not to be anymore.

I carry your face. You and I have talked about this many times after we have taken a picture together and looked at the photo. You will say, "Well, hon, you certainly are your mother's son. For better or worse, the older you get, you look like your momma." I am proud that I have taken on your features because we hold some of the same pain, the same darkness, caused by the same man.

I carry your stubbornness. Now, I often tease you about your famous stubbornness, but be mindful that it is enduring because it also can be defined as determination and grit. That stubbornness has helped me become resilient over the years and endure many struggles, so I have the ability to pick myself up, dust off my boots, and keep moving forward. It has also allowed me to put up walls when needed, though that is easier for a son to do than a mother at times.

It is true, I carry your depression and anxiety, and you carry mine. We are both very aware of the dark angels that come to greet us from time to time. They stand close, placing the heavy chains around our wrists and ankles, and make us look deep into our souls for what is causing the darkness to visit. It is something that I write and talk about, and have accepted is a part of me. In your eighty-four years, you have accepted it as well, which allows us to share with one another when our minds crawl through the mud of depression.

I carry many of your values. I may have gotten off course in my life, and that is okay, because I now realize that we all must drift off our path in order to experience all that life has to offer, good and bad. However, my value system has always been sound and has grown as I have tried to develop myself and continue on my own journey. One of the greatest experiences that you gave me as a child, which built a strong foundation, was helping you at the nursing home where you worked. To be around older people, especially people that are in their last stages of life, started to build a base of compassion and empathy. It also built a foundation of wanting to hear their spoken word and listen to stories. Our old people have so much wisdom to offer us. The respect you demanded from us towards old people came naturally. I often have thought that what you did for us, keeping us near old people, sometimes pushing them in their wheelchairs, helping them take a sip of water, and simply listening to them, should be a required class in school for all young people. However, I was lucky enough to have a mother who knew that the school was not responsible for my upbringing, so she took it upon herself to lay the groundwork.

I carry some of your weight on my shoulders. It is what good sons do for their mothers.

I carry so much of you with me, and I will always carry it all, for the remainder of my life, and do it with pride. At your celebration of life last weekend, when I stood up to say a few words, I spoke about your teachings and legacy. I mentioned how I do not have my own children, but I have hundreds upon hundreds that I have encountered through my work. All of my former students, from when I was a teacher and an administrator, will carry you with them as well, and without ever knowing it. I have included you in all of my teachings to them. Certainly, there was no set curriculum, but to me, most of the best teaching comes from life experiences, values, humility, and building sound integrity. My students now carry a part of you with them, and I am certain, they will place it on someone else's back along the way to carry along with them. That is your legacy. It will be carried on in ways that none of us will ever know.

I carry your love. I always will.

Love,

Chuck

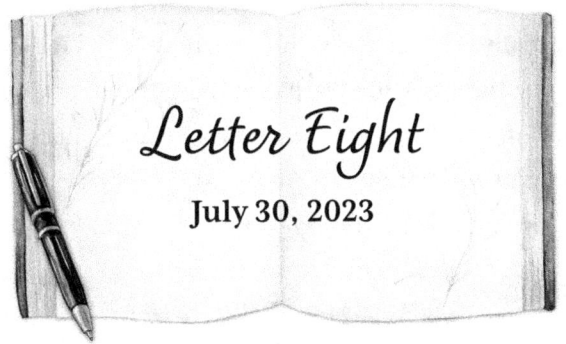

Letter Eight

July 30, 2023

Dear Mom,

I sat across from you recently and said, "I am grieving, this is true, but you are also grieving as well." It is something that I have been reflecting on and as I see the darkness in your eyes every so often, a darkness that we both carry, one of depression and at times, inner turmoil, I have thought about your personal grieving. We often think the only ones grieving are the people who are witnessing the death of a loved one. Yet, I am not sure how often we think about what the dying may be going through and how they are coping with the loss of themselves and the people and things they will miss. So, as I often do, I asked you a hard question, opening up the door to a genuine, heartfelt response, because I wanted to give you a space to talk about your own grieving.

"Mom, you are also grieving. I know you recognize this?"

You nodded, "Yes, I certainly am."

"What are you grieving for the most?"

"That I will not be here with all of y'all. I will miss my family."

This response brought your life's purpose to the forefront again. You are many things: A poet, a painter, a philosopher in your own right, a worker, and a warrior. However, I believe what has trumped everything, and what has given you the determination to fight your entire life is your kids and the extensions of them.

"What else will you miss?" I asked.

"My family is the most important thing to me, and I will miss my Dixie. Like all dogs, she has been my saving grace, my companion."

I have been learning about death from you. These are things I knew about you and I put to practice in my own life, but I didn't hear you say that you will miss material items like a television, phone, or the gossip from a neighbor. I didn't hear you say that you will miss social media or negative people. There was nothing in our conversation about grieving where you said you would miss anything that was not of significance. It was mostly about missing the love that you have in your life.

Watching this unfold, anticipating when you will move into the next phase of dying, when our conversations will be limited or taken away altogether, I feel the need to ask you more and more questions, mostly because I know it is good to talk about and for you to process.

I have sat and wondered some of these questions myself: How would I respond if I was told I had two months to live? What would I want my time left to look and feel like? What would I be grieving for and what would I miss? Have I said and done what I needed to? Have I had the conversations that will help me move onto the next realm, and the conversations that will help the people I love come to peace?

There are so many questions to be asked and answered.

I know this, and I have for some years now, I will live life on my terms, to the fullest. That means I will embrace joy and I will accept the suffering that life will bring. It also means that I will worry about what is within my control and let go of what is not, and with that removing as much toxicity from my life as I can. There really is no place for such people, places, or things. Life is far too precious and short to waste any moments, where your peace may be taken from the absent-minded folks, or from circumstances that you have no control over. Worrying about what might happen, or what hasn't even happened yet, making up situations in our minds, instead of being in the present moment, is the cause of much anxiety.

I have protected myself as much as I can when I find I am wading in the poisonous pond of negative circumstances. It has caused me to put on my armor and leave places of work, relationships, and certain events behind. It has prompted me to remove myself for my own sanity and health, which can take a lot of work and sacrifice. However, it is worth it. So, when I ask you about what you will miss or your own grieving as a dying woman, it makes me think of how I would answer those same questions. It makes me want to live my life by how I would answer them.

In reflection of my own questions that I asked you, placing myself in your well-worn shoes, I have some answers. As I age, I would grieve my loss of independence and my health. I would grieve my ailing body and not being able to walk the trails and witness the deer run through the deep woods. Therefore, I must continue to move, be mobile, and build my aging body so that it will last. I want to be deep into my eighties and still feel the trails beneath my feet, for the woods offer solace. It offers peace away from a spinning world full of busy ants and grazing sheep. I would miss the taste of good food and wine, and seeing the sunset just below the bluffs and the tops of trees or a mountain peak. I would miss hearing the laughter of my nieces and nephews and seeing them grow into the people they will become. I would miss seeing foreign lands and contemplating if we could live there and start a new chapter of life. I would miss hearing the shuffle of my students coming into a classroom to tell me how they are doing and allowing me in their lives just enough so that I could help guide them if needed. I would miss the smell of wildflowers and the warmth of my dogs laying against me. I would miss my fingers on a keyboard trying like hell to connect with my mind and then articulate the thoughts onto a blank page. Mostly, I would miss my love. I would miss our conversations and talking about our dreams. I would miss holding her hand and when she takes her hand and places it on my arm as we walk. I would miss making love. I would miss dancing with her and laughing at our improvisational moves, and I would miss experiencing all that life has to offer with the person that I find more interesting and more beautiful as each year passes. There is a lot I would miss, and by answering that question, the question I have for my dying mother, I have answered how I want to live my life. It is the simple things that really aren't so simple because they make up what is meaningful to me. Therefore, I hold them tight, guarded, so that no one can disrupt what I have and will build, which makes what I have mentioned complex and not simple. Hanging onto what we truly love about life in a world that can be so disruptive can be difficult at times. Love itself is so complex because it creates so much emotion.

Mom, know this: I will miss you. I know that I can shut my eyes and see you or hear your voice whenever I want. Actually, your voice is something I have recorded and will save it for my lifetime. I will miss our conversations, knowing that I have always trusted you. I cherish knowing that I have trusted you since I was a child and will miss it because trust is sacred. I have been grieving for you for a long time and will continue to grieve for a lifetime. That is okay because grieving means that you have loved me and I have loved you.

I will miss your hugs. That is something that I will no longer experience. The power of human touch, the love and protection of a mother, it is something I will miss.

For you, I want you to know that while you will miss me, you will be just a thought away. You will be the butterfly on a sunflower, and you will be the shiniest star in the sky. You will be the soft breeze that for some odd reason is in a sealed room and it causes me goosebumps, and you will be the shiny rock that has no earthly business being on a wooded trail. You will be the orange glow in the setting sun, and you will be the words that fill a page. I will miss you but you will never leave me and therefore I will never leave you. So let's grieve together and allow our tears to flow on one another's shoulders.

Love,

Chuck

Letter Nine

August 4, 2023

Dear Mom,

I have found that looking at a calendar has a new meaning. When your oncologist said, "Two months," I immediately came home and mapped out the weeks. Of course, no one knows the exact date, but as Karen tells me, I am always thinking of the big picture, letting details fall to the side for the moment, wanting to understand where I am headed. In this case, where we are headed.

I look at a calendar and wonder when your decline will start for real? There is a reality that sits in front of you and your family, and that is there will be a moment that you will not be able to rise from your bed, get dressed, take care of your needs, and possibly not verbally communicate. There will also be the time when all communication comes to a halt, but you will still hear my voice. I promise that I will read you poems and tell you about the trails I hiked and the color of the sunset because I know you will hear me.

The great anticipation of what will come has caused me to ask the question of sacrifice. That word has recently caused a stir, but what the conditioned minds did not see or ask was that I was asking myself, am I ready? Am I ready to sacrifice what is needed in order to send you off with dignity? I often ask myself such questions to become prepared. It's like when I climb a mountain peak or start a long run, or when I am already injured and decide to tackle the physical obstacles ahead of me. The same question arises when I wake up to the darkness of depression. I know the torment of what my mind is capable of when my light fades for a while, so I need to ask myself if I am ready to battle it. "Am I ready for the pain?" I asked myself the same question when I started graduate school or any other endeavor. So, to prepare, I needed to pose this question to myself and others, "Are we ready?" It seemed like a legitimate question and one that requires reflection. Perhaps, asking the high price of self-reflection was my mistake?

Time does not slow. There are twenty-four hours in the day and seven days in the week and thirty-one or less days in the month. And, there are approximately sixty-one days in two months. A two-month prognosis woke me up once again to time, that uncompromising bastard. So, when will time end for you? When will it come and take your voice away from us? When will you no longer be able to hug me back? When will your eyes close but your chest still rise with shallow breaths?

Most deaths I have been near have been rapid, tragic, and hurried by God. They have been from suicide and being shot by the police. They have been sudden with a loss of internal systems and "stomach strokes." They have been an intentional medical suicide from a cowardly man who could have lived well but decided he was too lazy to care for himself. I have not witnessed very many slow deaths. Though, I will say that all death is tragic, there is nothing beautiful about dying slow or fast. Yet, I am finding when I look at the calendar, I am grateful. I am grateful that I have the time to spend with you, to say a few things that a son must in order to find as much peace as possible. I find gratitude in the moments where I have gotten to take a ride in the country with my brother and you and listen to your stories from the backseat. The slowness of your death has given me a gift that I want to take advantage of without being too intrusive of your time. As we discussed, the dying need alone time as well. You need time to process what is happening and grieve in private. I would want the same, and am actually doing so myself, taking time alone to just sit with death.

We do need to be careful of our attachment to life. We are all impermanent. Our life, as does our youth, will eventually vanish. The turning calendar is the great dictator of wrinkled skin and shallow breaths. It does not frighten me. It makes me curious and want to live the life I choose. I am uncompromising when it comes to living my way, and often that leads to the path of self-discovery through self-awareness, one where I explore my past, strive to be in the present, and map out a future that I hope will leave something for those who will listen. My hope is that they listen with open ears to the message I am delivering to help their own minds heal. At the very least, if not complete healing (some wounds stay open), to learn to cope and accept. To build resilience to their darkness and anxieties, and the obstacles that will come their way. Life is a series of obstacles being rushed by a ticking clock.

When the calendar turned to August, I cried. August is a month for me to remember dates. It is when I entered basic training so long ago, thirty-four years to be exact. For some, that is a lifetime. It is when my best friend took his life. Oh, how I wish I could be with him again and have the wisdom I have now, but I was only thirty-four when he died, and mindfulness, empathy, and compassion were not in my vocabulary. Though, as the Stoics say, he had to "open the door." August is when I question if I am ready for another year of teaching. Do I have it in me? Teaching is one of the best things I ever did for myself, but have my edges become too crisp? I am tired, weary at times, of the politics and recycled nature of education. It seems as if we are often spinning our wheels year after year with the same issues and same conversations without real change or improvement. Can I do it again for another school year? My virtues are tested with each passing month. So, when I saw August first arrive, I cried. I cried because if Mother Time is correct, this is the month that we may see you start to progress to the end. Am I ready? The beast of time does not stop. We must smile upon it because it will continue to give and take, and the beast is hungry. It wants to feast.

I have studied, and more importantly, put into practice what I have been learning from the philosophy of Stoicism, to understand what is and is not in my control. I know, dear mother, that I cannot control your death, just as I could not control your cancer. I cannot control the calendar turning to August and the daunting ticking of the clock. It is not for me to decide when you will give your last hug or your last breath. In fact, I would not want such power or capabilities. It would be too great of a responsibility to make those decisions or choices. I do not control how others act or respond. What I do control is my own actions and my response to what is happening and the

46

choices I make. I choose how I want to respond to the chaos of life. For example, these letters to you. They have raised some eyebrows and questions from folks with blurred vision, but they have mostly reached people who have also cried when the calendar turns. Many readers can relate to the mourning of an anniversary date. They have seen the monster that time can be, how it wants to devour what's in its path, and how time will make us all grieve eventually. I know this to be true, I will eventually mourn another date on the calendar.

We can either look at time as a restless beast, out to torment us, or we can be grateful for each moment. I leave these words to ponder. I have decided that focusing on gratitude is the way I want to live my life. I have also decided long ago that it is okay to digest grief within the belly of time. It is okay to mourn a specific date, and a certain smell or picture that reminds you of a great loss that you may have experienced. It is all life, and life is full of emotion that changes like the hands on a clock. Life is to be lived well and that is defined differently for all of us. I have written out what that means for me and I study the definition daily, trying to capture it all, because life is extraordinary and time is a generous gift, wrapped in colorful paper and a fragile box.

Love,

Chuck

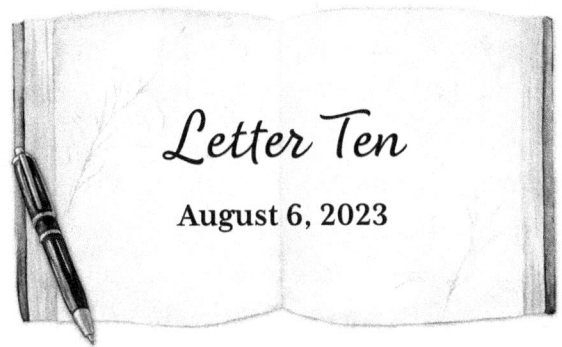

Letter Ten

August 6, 2023

Dear Mom,

I am having one of those moments when life seems daunting and I am weary. It is not just your dying. Of course, that is part of it, but it is life itself and the pressures I place against my own temples. It is one of those times that seem to be more frequent the past few years, where I want to disappear from the world and wander. Remove myself and search for nothing except the beauty of a mountain landscape and good conversation.

These moments like to test me, as they have you for most of your life. Depression tests us in different ways because it is not an argument or toxic situation that we can simply walk away from. It is us, and we must face ourselves fully. It is like standing naked in the mirror and looking at all of your so-called "flaws." Except this is a mental mirror, and instead of picking apart all of our physical features that we may despise, it is our mind and memory that we feel is not worthy.

In my twenties, I thought my depression was an inherited madness from a man that had once tormented me physically and mentally. However, I would never let my hate for him sit on my shoulders, controlling my emotions so long after his death, so I forgave him. Oh, mother, I had to forgive him because my forgiveness would show that I am stronger than he ever was. My forgiveness is for me, taking back control of my life. I have concluded that my depression is an inherited sadness. It is something that runs deep across generations, but it is far from madness.

You have talked to me about your depression for years. It is something we share. When you meet someone who knows that kind of darkness and mental pain, you connect in a different way, whether they are a parent, family member, friend, student, or even a stranger that you have a brief encounter with. It is a shared pain. They do not need to say much more than, "My depression arrived this morning," for you to understand the torment and obstacles that they are facing. As a fellow depressive, you realize what they will be battling: the invisible enemy that is visible to a fellow sufferer. It is the same when I speak at events to people about depression and anxiety. There is a common bond in the crowd where you know, at least a little, of what the other person is going through. Even though everyone's depression and anxiety are different, there are enough similarities to have a great deal of understanding and empathy for the other person.

I see your depression. It is there, sitting on both of your shoulders, and how could it not? I talk to you openly about your depression and your grieving for what you have lost and what you will be losing. It is okay to have that darkness and it does not have to be carried alone. I see your darkness sitting on your eyelids and weighing down your spine where the cancer mostly lives, causing you a great deal of suffering. What suffers more, I sometimes wonder, your body or your mind? It's okay to not be okay! I scream that shit in my head all the time when I see people try to conceal their pain, their feelings, and depression. None of us need to be okay all the time. It's called life, and we will all be alright if we just take a moment to understand one another, but more importantly, understand ourselves.

I do not apologize for my tears or for my emotional scars, and neither should you. We all have this line we feel compelled to say after tears fall, and that is, "I'm sorry." Why? Why be sorry for being human? For having emotion? I have found purpose in my life, and that is spreading the message that you do not need to apologize for your depression or anxiety. You do not need to apologize for your tears or being in this human experiment we call life.

I left your apartment Friday and smiled at Karen, telling her, "I am sure going to miss her."

I am here to help hold your darkness until you finally let go. I am here to help you through your last days and find understanding and reason in your pain.

I came home today from my bike ride and wept. I needed to because the world is heavy at times. My blessing and curse is that I am a true empath. I feel everything. I often tell my students that I can feel all of their energy, problems, and emotions the moment they enter my classroom. It has allowed me to help them, but many days it is a heavy weight to carry. I feel the same with friends, and I see and feel it in you. You can never cover up your emotions or the weight of your life and your dying. I feel it all, and that is okay because I am strong and can bear the weight on my back. It is why I have strengthened my mind and body for my entire life, to lift what I carry as well as those around me.

I am going to miss you. I have told you this. I know you will always be close. You will be the white butterfly that flows next to me on the trail, and you will be the smell of chicken and dumplings. You will be the breeze that warms my face on a June day, and you will be the hawk feather I see lying in the middle of the woods. Perhaps, when it is my time to go, to leave this world, you will be the hand that comes for me to lead me to that next path. I will miss you, but I know you will be there, a thought away, when I am struggling in my mind.

That is all I have for today, for it is enough to sit in the darkness in broad daylight. It is time to rest.

Love,
Chuck

Letter Eleven

August 10, 2023

Dear Mom,

I was sitting next to you recently on your patio, and you brought up an old story, one that I told you about a few years ago, but goes back forty-five years. It was when an eight-year-old boy was frightened that you were leaving for a few nights. You couldn't have known why I was so scared, but that does not matter now. I am not that eight-year-old boy but a fifty-three-year-old man, with a gray shade of whiskers lining my face, and a few wrinkles on the sides of my eyes showing that I have lived a good life. I never hide my age. I wear experience with pride.

You looked at me and Karen and talked about how I used to cuddle up next to you as a child and lay by you while we watched television. You said I was always sensitive, affectionate, and showed emotion. The story goes that when I was eight years old and you were packed to go on a short trip, I went into your suitcase and found a pair of your ankle-high socks and took them from your suitcase. It was my attempt to keep you with me. A cotton safety shield that would protect me. I carried your socks with me every day to school in my pocket. Now, I am certain that this would have generated much laughter if the other kids in my class knew what I was holding. It may have even appeared strange to my teacher if she would have seen the balled-up pair of socks. However, if they would have known the significance that they had for that week, I am certain they would have understood why I carried them with me. In my childlike mind, I figured if I had your socks that you would have to return. I needed something of yours to be close to. It was a reminder that you would be back to hold me again during a time when a father's rage was in battle with a mother's love. Love won! It always has because love is the most powerful emotion we possess.

After you amusingly, and I would say proudly, retold the story, you said, "Honey," and you patted my arm as I sat next to you with the warm August breeze filtering through the space we held on your patio, "Go into my closet and get yourself a pair of my socks and take them with you."

We all smiled at this. Certainly, it is a sweet story about a boy who loved his mother more than life itself, and now a slightly more than middle-aged man who sits beside her as she is dying, talking about stealing a pair of socks. So, as I went into your apartment while you and Karen talked, I took a pair of your socks and I have put them in a place where I keep a few sacred items. They will be next to me as I write my stories. It is the little things in life that are often enormous.

I will always hold you close. The protectiveness of the cotton armor that I carry will be near, reminding me of how much I love you and how if you would not have returned from your trip that year, in the spring of 1978, I am not sure I would have survived what was happening. The socks are a symbol of resilience, closeness, memory, and warmth. Your socks have meaning.

It is August 10th. One month and three days ago, we were told you had two months. Time does not stop for love. It doesn't slow down, even just a little. That is okay because it is a great reminder. A ticking tune that sings in our ears that this life is precious and we must live it well, accepting all that life has to offer and, when the time inevitably comes, also accepting death.

Love,

Chuck

Letter Twelve

August 11, 2023

Dear Mom,

The day is fragile. Each moment in each day has meaning. We get to decide what we do with it. We decide how we want to live this life. For me, I will continue to find great joy in walking the trails, writing, and looking into the eyes of the person I love. I have found that I do not need much in life and that I am content, happy even, with simple things. I find joy in experiences and meaningful conversations. I find it in watching sunsets and being grateful when I get to breathe fresh air, see a dog's tail wag, and hear the voices of the people I love. When I get to help another person through their tough times, I find purpose and meaning. I tell you this because as you start this next phase of dying, the phase where I believe you will start to let go, I want you to know that I will be okay. You have raised a strong, resilient son, who knows exactly who he is. To be self-aware enough to know oneself well and true brings a great deal of confidence and joy.

Last Sunday you said to me that you are tired. You were not talking about the exhaustion that cancer has brought to your body and mind. You were speaking of being tired and close to being ready to depart this world. You keep saying, "But I am still fighting." I then took the chance to say, "Mom, if you need one of your kids to say this to you, I will be the one." I paused for a moment, "If you need to let go, it is okay. It is okay to leave us if you are ready. You have suffered enough and you are tired. We will be okay."

This was not easy for me to say to you, but I feel that we sometimes have to say the hard things in case they are the right things. We need to be selfless when it comes to death.

I heard you justify your dying, saying that you are eighty-four years old and it is unrealistic to expect to live forever, and that your kids will also grow old one day and die as well. To me, this is what I have talked to you about before, and attempted to remind others and myself, that you too are grieving. You grieve for all that you have and will be losing.

Our conversation went from letting go, to the idea that we are all impermanent and owe a death. The truest thing one can say is, "I will someday die."

Today, as we sat in oncology talking to your wonderful doctor, telling us that many of your levels are too high, it showed us again what we are facing. I say "we" because you are not dying alone. You have the strength of those you delivered into this world walking beside you. Yet, as I asked the doctor if two months is still the reality, she said, "Yes, it is," and that was over a month ago. We like our cards lying face up on the table, don't we? When I asked what this will look like going forward, she replied, "With your potassium levels being what they are, you could have heart failure tonight." Yes, the cards are facing up, and she just flipped a joker.

This is the great mystery about death, that no one really knows the exact date that it will happen, so it could be two months or it could be tonight.

We had a discussion about normalizing talking about death. I believe this with my whole beating heart, that we should talk about dying while we are young and healthy. We should also talk about aging. Why would we not? It is just another phase of life. It will happen, so why not prepare for it? Perhaps we should have mentors that can guide us all as we age and move closer to dying. Part of the problem in our society is that we celebrate youth as if we will always have it. This cannot happen, and we should not want it to. We try to hang onto something that will fade, so why not do so with grace? I sit here now beyond my middle age, beyond that youthful part of my life, celebrating the current path that I am on. I have studied aging and death for years. It is why I do not fear either one. You helped prepare me for that. If I am lucky, I will be an old man, walking the woods and this earth, curious as to what is next, and passing as much wisdom and knowledge on to whomever will listen.

You are now on a pilgrimage, one that will end either in darkness and nothing, or in heaven. Many of us are brought up to believe something else is out there, but you will soon get to see for yourself. You have to be curious as to what is next, and that is why it's okay to let go.

As we have discussed, there has to be more. We know this because we have shared stories that can only be explained by having the belief in the heavens and angels. The presence of those who have died before us has been near, so near that our eyes have seen them in passing. A year and a half ago, the day before I approached the darkness myself, Charlotte came to me in a dream, though I am still unsure if it was a dream or reality. One could say it was the cocktail of pain meds that clouded my brain, but it was too real not to be something larger than myself. At first, I thought I had died and she was guiding me to wherever it is she has been the past thirteen years, but I now believe she was guiding me back to life. I was lucky that day to turn off the key. An angel found me and wanted me to keep walking my path in this life. I will walk it with sturdy boots.

Letting go is a gift I have taught myself. I have learned to let go of things that I cannot control. What I do control is how I treat others and how I respond to their actions. I control how I want to conduct myself in this life and what I do with the moments that I have. Yes, sometimes those moments are challenged. They are interrupted by the difficulties that we face in life or by people that struggle to be happy for others. Whatever may be the circumstance, I can choose my own virtues and what I value. Letting go and reframing my thoughts and situations has offered me a way of looking at life that has helped me brush the cracked concrete off my shoulders and shackles from my ankles. Letting go has given me freedom to stand for what I believe in and, for the most part, choosing who I want to keep company with. Letting go is powerful and a gift we can give to ourselves. You, dear mother, cannot control dying, and you cannot control your suffering. You cannot control leaving your children or your dog. What is within your control is what you are doing, which is grappling with cancer, showing strength, and dignity. You have reflected on your life and your death and are now admitting that you are, "Just about ready." It is okay to be ready to die. You are a warrior that will walk on a greater path. You are an explorer that is about to go on a journey where you will discover truths beyond this world. All I ask is that you come back to visit every so often.

Yes, the day is fragile, but it is also wonderful.

Love,

Chuck

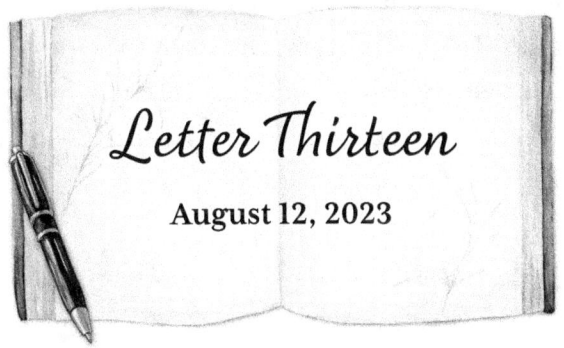

Letter Thirteen

August 12, 2023

Dear Mom,

You told me to never hide my emotions about your dying, and I haven't. I hesitantly left your apartment yesterday, wondering if I would see you again. When the oncologist said your potassium levels are at a point where you could have heart failure at any time, it was another wake-up call to the reality that sits beside us. So, when I left you as you were getting ready to rest, Dixie on your lap, I took a second glance, wondering if this is it.

There is a heaviness in my chest, like a pressure of someone greater than myself pushing their palm against it, right in the middle where the bone is a shield to my heart. However, this type of ache no shield can protect. The anticipation of when you will leave often makes a tingling wave of sensations across my skin. I know you need your rest, but when Karen came home last night and I told her about your appointment, I said, "I hope I am there with her. It is becoming harder to leave her, and I hope I am with her when she goes."

I went to sleep and turned my phone's volume high and kept it near with this strange thought that maybe you would call and tell me, "Hon, it's time. C'mon over." How naive I am about death to think it would be like that. As if you would have the energy to pick up your phone, call me, and predict the time of your departure. Maybe it's the writer in me, trying to find the perfect ending.

I feel this great need to hold onto you and let you go all at once. I am in an internal boxing match, sending left hooks and uppercuts to my soul and conscience, and my fatigue is setting in because it is the fifteenth round. However, you are a fighter and you raised a fighter. We bow to no one, and this has caused me to have a straight spine and strong shoulders, but heavy arms and a tired mind. I will keep fighting, but I am weary. I ache watching your pain. Each time you sigh, I do too. I wish I could give you all of my strength just one time. I wish you could be pain-free for just one day before you go so that you can remember what it was like to have an able body. Though once again, I am being naive. You have had pain most of your life. That is life. It is full of pain and suffering, and that is why we must learn how to navigate it and be mindful of our joy. I know your joy; it is in your children's eyes and seeing your grandchildren walk through the door. It is in a dog that loves you unconditionally and in your writing and painting. Your joy is greater than your pain. Oh, mother, I need you to remember that. You have had a wonderful, joyous life. It has been worthwhile. I will make my life worthwhile and extraordinary because you gave me this life to do so, and I will not disappoint. I will walk this earth to make a difference.

You said to me yesterday, "I have learned more in the past two years than I have in the last twenty." Your illness and pain have taught you a lot. It was another lesson in how resilient you are. It has taught you about yourself in ways that you never knew possible. It has also taught you about the people around you. We learn when we are uncomfortable, and well, I could not imagine being more uncomfortable than having cancer of the bone. What a cruel son of a bitch it has been, but you didn't succumb. You fought and never kneeled. Your oncologist said that you have lived this long because of your grit. She went on to say, "We do not see this very often. This type of will and determination to fight." The will to fight! Yes, it is what I often say when I am writing or talking about depression and anxiety. One must build resilience and have the will to fight. Thank you for teaching me.

My fingers have become tired from typing words that have led to tears. I crumble and turn into a child when I think of losing you. It's okay, I will stand tall again as a man who understands life and death, and himself, but it feels right to break every so often. It feels real.

Love,

Chuck

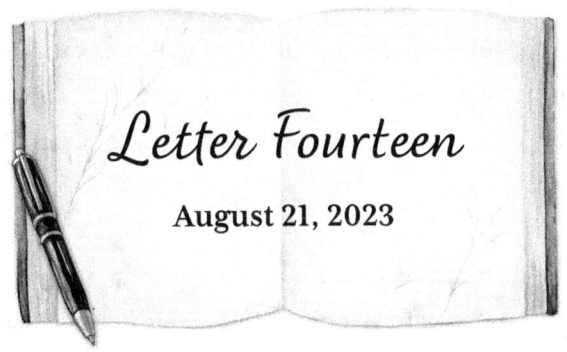

Letter Fourteen

August 21, 2023

Dear Mom,

You recently told me that you have learned a lot from me over the years and said, "I have been listening." I am thankful that you were listening. It is okay for a child to teach a parent, especially when that instruction is meant to help them live a better life. I share little bits of myself or the knowledge and wisdom that I have gained from setbacks in my life in order to help others. That is, if people are ready to listen. I have never claimed to have all the answers. I just have experiences that I am willing to share and hope that others can relate and it can help relieve the pain that is trapped in their mind. For you, I have simply tried to teach you about being mindful and also letting go of what you cannot control.

We have often spoken about our relationship with Dad. He is someone who is difficult to dissect, and though we have different stories of the harm he caused, there is also an understanding between us of the fear he brought. As I have mentioned many times,

I had to find forgiveness for him because it gave me back control of what he tried to take. Forgiveness was for me. I keep repeating that as a reminder to stop hating him. I also had to understand that I could not control anything that he did or said to me. However, as an adult, as a fifty-three-year-old man, I have the ability to control how I now respond to his abuse.

We have also talked about our family. Your immediate family is, of course, your children, but it is also your parents and siblings. Something that I have repeated for years is that we do not get to choose our family. We were born into it and had to make the best of it during our younger years. Yet, our society seems to have this harmful dialogue of "Blood is thicker than water." Our discussions have always led to me replying to that statement with, "...but to what detriment?" I think many times this was difficult for you to hear because you are loyal to your parents and want your children to have a relationship with one another. However, if we do not like our family members or do not hold similar values, or if they cause us stress and create toxicity in our lives, then why should we continue to engage with them? To me, this has never made sense, and so as a son, I had to share this so that you can reconcile your own stress that your family, my extended family, has caused. This is okay. We do not need to stay in any environment that causes us to lose our peace. Mostly, I have tried to teach you how to be in the present moment and let go of what you cannot control. To realize that being negative about something or someone does not change anything, so why not find happiness and calmness?

Lately, I have heard you talk a lot about your family and dad, and relive, reevaluate, and try to make sense of the happenings and relationships in your life. This, from what I understand, is normal at the end of life. It does make sense to rehash it all. However, what I have encouraged you to do is finally find forgiveness in those things that you had no control over. You were just a kid when you got married and started having babies. It is time to let all of it go. Wherever you are heading, it doesn't matter anymore. The strife and pain that was brought to you throughout your life is ending. I believe it is crucial to find peace while living. It is important to go wherever or whatever that next place is with a calm mind and heart. That is a valuable lesson for all of us, to find peace and forgiveness in our lives while we are here, healthy, and have years to live. Letting go of the things that we had no control over liberates us and offers a great deal of freedom. This world is full of people with their own agendas, some ethical and many not, and their egos control them and therefore they want to control others. I have never hung around when I have been in situations where people have conducted themselves this way, whether it directly affected me or impacted everyone as a whole. I had to outweigh the cost of not letting much grass grow under my feet or leave negative relationships, to taking care of my own mental health and staying true to my virtues. It can be a hard road to travel at times but I think it's worth it.

With saying all of this, it has been important for you to tell your stories to us all. If we listened, if we have been good students, you have been our greatest teacher. When we recently sat on your porch and you started to tell the stories that have made up your life, your train of thought often paused and you lost what you were saying. You knew it was happening and said, "It is so frustrating to forget what I am saying." I encourage you to give yourself grace. I told you that you were either going to be distracted by the extreme pain that you have been in for the past two and a half years or the morphine that is flowing through your veins. Pain has a peculiar way of either taking away our thoughts or making them more clear. Pain can offer an extreme alertness to the world around us. In that way, suffering is a gift. However, when I sat with you yesterday and you said, "I have no pain after my morphine was increased," I nearly welled up in tears. As your son, I have a great need to protect you, I always have, and to see you in pain has caused a pressure on my temples and heaviness on my shoulders. I wish I could have taken it all from you, the pain and discomfort, and given you some respite. However, I have no control over that, but those little pills do. Yes, you lost many of your words and they were scattered, but I have not seen you so relaxed since cancer decided to torment you.

So, dear mother, if you want another lesson from your son, be comfortable. I sat across from you and said, "Mom, you do not have to remember all of your stories. Your children know them all and can be your memory for you. The important thing is that you do not feel any pain. You deserve that." I believe that was difficult for you to hear. I have told you this before, but it has always seemed to me that you thought you deserved pain in your life, physical and emotional. It's as if you felt you needed to carry all of your suffering alone and just take it. I understand this thought because I have been there, but it is not a thought that holds truth. Neither of us deserves pain. What we deserve is to find peace within our minds and understand what happened to us was an important part of our life that helped shape our resilience, but it has never defined who we are. We are in control of writing our own definition of who we truly are and how we respond to life. How do I define you? You are a remarkable woman who has defied many odds in her life and created stories that will live well past your years. You are an artist, a mother, and a storyteller.

I too am losing my thoughts, and I am not sure I want to go back and read and edit this jumbled mess I just produced. I was sitting on my couch last week and looked at Karen and said, "I feel like I have the flu." She pulled up a list of physical symptoms of grieving, and I put a checkmark next to every damn one of them. My therapist concurred. I tell you this because you are not alone. I, like all of your children and grandchildren, am grieving your loss with you. That is what you have created, a family that has the commonality to grieve for your loss. For better or for worse, grieving is something that we all will have to face at some point in our lives. The response to how we grieve is also within our control, and it is perpetual. After you lose someone you love, grieving lasts a lifetime, and we learn how to control our reaction to it so that we can go on living life.

I will go on living my life and will offer much of it as a tribute to you. Let me take a moment and tell you what is to come for your youngest. It's important for me that you know I will be okay and I will go on to accomplish what I set out to do. I will write more novels; two are already in the making. I will continue to bring awareness to mental illness through writing and speaking. I plan on taking many journeys for the remainder of my life and walk among ancient cities, beautiful beaches, and mountain trails. I will keep teaching and maybe do so at the college level. Mostly, I will continue loving a woman and spending the rest of my days at her side. To love someone so strongly, with all my might, and for her to know she is loved and knowing that she loves me back is the greatest accomplishment. I am a fortunate man. I had the good fortune to be your son.

Thank you for allowing me to teach you a few things along the way. It takes humility to be a good student.

Love,

Chuck

Letter Fifteen

August 22, 2023

Dear Mom,

I woke up this morning, not a man but a frightened child, startled by a dream about you. It was strange as I lay there breathing heavily, feeling as if I could not lift my arms, and I looked around the room for you. It was as if I was transported back to my seven-year-old body, looking through seven-year-old eyes, and wanting to scream out for you.

After I placed my hands on my face, trying to rub away the feeling of helplessness, I felt the light beard that covered my chin and realized I was not the child seeking his mother for comfort, but the man who is grieving for her. A man who realizes that time is running out.

After I shook the hazy fog from my head, I looked at my phone to see the date piercing back at me. Oh, the haunting whisper of the calendar. It is August 22nd. What does that mean? Well, to many I know right now, it means that school is starting soon, so it is time to start complaining that summer is almost over. Some will complain they have grown another year older, and then others will just let the day pass mindlessly because it is a Tuesday and they just want Friday to hurry so they can have off, doing whatever it is they do over the weekend. I am sure others in the world are also looking at their phones and realize that a turning calendar is one less day with their mom. Perspective on how we look at a calendar is interesting. Living mindfully, in the moment, seems best. Complaints are a waste of breath, which means they are a waste of life. Why complain about something that is not in your control? Complaining is a common dialogue for many, and maybe it brings them comfort and security because it is familiar to them?

For me, when I looked at the date, I scrolled ahead looking to when September 7th would come. That would be two months. That would be the timeline you were given. However, I keep saying two months when your doctor said two or three. I guess that's the pessimist coming out of me. It's difficult to examine our minds at times and realize that not every thought is fed by optimism. However, how can one be optimistic about death? I enjoy being my worst critic. It helps me become more self-aware and attempt to improve.

The anticipation of your decline is sticking to my ribs and causing a churning stomach. For certain, we have had our moments where we wondered, "Is this it?" As I told your grandson on the phone last night, "She's a tough ol' gal. If you look under the definition of grit, it is a picture of your grandma looking back with determination."

The anticipation is a beast at times. However, as I spoke to my therapist last week and talked to him about how I was handling your decline, he commented, "You are doing very well by accepting it all. It seems as if you have had the conversations you need to with your mom, and that is good." He is right, I am handling all of this to the best of my ability. We have had important conversations that a mother and son should have as death lingers above us all. Still, for two people like us that have the gift of gab, there is never enough time to say everything.

You too, more than any of us, are anticipating when all of this will come to fruition. You have to be curious, wondering what will finally be the moment that you will draw your last breath? I know I would be. It is something I sometimes wonder when my mind drifts. How will I die?

We have been fortunate to have this time. I am certain that some would think a quick death is best, and some might think a slow, lingering one is the way to go. I know there are others that don't want to think about death at all or even avoid the thought that they will die. It is good to have a date, a timeline, ahead of us. We like to know what we're facing so we have time to throw some stories around. For me, and I think I can comfortably say, for us, death is a part of life. That is something you have prepared us for since we were young. Maybe it's why I woke up as my seven-year-old self was looking for you? I needed a mother's comfort to tell me that death was all a part of this journey. When I calmed my breath after waking and realizing I was a man, not a child, I heard your words, "Don't fear it, son. Not even my death. Don't fear what you cannot control."

I kicked up some dust on the trail last night and smiled at the falling sun. You were there.

Love,
Chuck

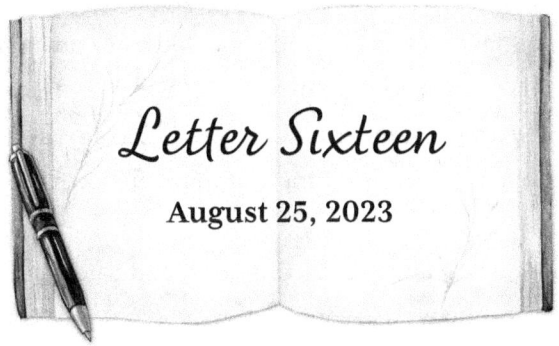

Letter Sixteen

August 25, 2023

Dear Mom,

Well, I am sitting here next to you, lady, watching you sleep. It looks like you've taken a turn for the worse and ended up here in hospice care. The doctor told Carl you are dying. It's what we've been waiting for, I guess, but no one, if they are telling the truth, is truly ready for death.

I arrived here yesterday morning at about 3:45 a.m. I was up in the north woods looking for answers among the trees and drove the four and a half hours to get to you. You woke up shortly after I sat next to you and said, "I wouldn't die. I wouldn't let them take me." You repeated the same thing over and over, startling those around you, but I had a sense of pride, knowing that you told death to wait a little longer. Later that afternoon when we were alone, you had tears literally falling from your eyes down your pretty face, and those tears told a story. I sat there holding your hand and you said a few things in between the sadness. One was that I reminded you of your daddy the way I sat and tilted my head and shoulders. Then you told me you didn't die because you were waiting for me to get there. You said, "I needed to see all my children." I asked if you had anyone else to see and you said that you saw everyone and you were now ready. I told you through a few tears of my own that it was okay to let go now. I believe you heard the same from Carl today. It's okay, sweet mother, it is time to stop fighting this thing and move on down the road.

You then talked a lot about Charlotte and said that she's been coming to visit you and there was a dim light and she was close. You always said when you die that Charlotte will come. I know there was some turmoil with that girl now and again, but you were meant to be her momma. You were meant to be the one who lifted her to be her best self and care for her while she walked this earth. She loved you and will guide you to wherever she has been. I'm certain of that.

I think about how much love you have had in this room the past couple of days. It has felt strong, genuine, and real. That is what you have built. It is a family that holds you up high. You said this evening before everyone left that you may be leaving. It is okay to leave us now. That day has come.

After the room cleared, you asked me to sit next to you. We talked about car rides and country air, and I told you it wasn't too late for me to put you in my truck and take you west until we saw some mountains. You gave me that look of yours and said, "You'd probably go find us a mountain lion." You may be right about that. I once told you that being taken by a mountain lion might just be a good death. "At least the damn thing would know he's been in a fight," I added. I'm not so sure about that anymore. I think a good death is being surrounded by people who love you. Yours will be a good one because of love.

Before you fell asleep, you asked me what I was going to do. When I told you I brought my computer with me, you said, "Oh, hon, can you sit next to me and write me a letter while I sleep?"

Well, Mom, it's time for your son to get a little more real. You won't read anymore of these letters, but I wouldn't ever hold back anyhow. If nothing else, I tell my truth. I am sitting here feeling helpless. As you know, I like to "fix" things. I like to try to lift you up from those bad places. There isn't a damn thing I can do about this. I am powerless to death. I heard you were hallucinating last night and having bad thoughts and dreams about Dad. He can't hurt you anymore. Yesterday you said to me, "I would have never let him hurt you if I had known." I know that, but this boy's back wasn't quite broken from his blows, so I kept quiet. I hate it that he still enters your nightmares. I can't fix that either. We share some pain, don't we? I then told you that I forgave him long ago because I am the better man. You liked that and agreed. Still, I sit here now and watch you sleep and look at your face lying sideways on the pillow, and I see pain. Not just from the past few years but a lifetime that has added up and held tight to the shine in your eyes. I want that pain to go away. It's hard for a son to want his mother to let go of life. It's like letting go of my own. However, it is the most loving thing I can do for you now, to encourage you to let go.

I am almost afraid to go to sleep. I listen to your breathing and don't want to miss the last one. However, there is also some peace knowing we will share the same air tonight. Our breath will mix, as will the beat of our hearts. The last breath. I'm not sure why I am thinking about something that no one knows when it will happen. No one can predict when that last breath will come. Someone will miss it or maybe everyone will. Death is hot tar on soft skin. It's a bee sting to the eyes, and it's a soothing, cool cloth on your face. Death is joyous and destructive and it's a celebration and a suffocation from a lead pillow. It brings so many emotions and all within three of your breaths, watching you lay there with an older version of my face.

I'm tired now. I think I will just lay back here in this chair, close to you, and fall asleep listening to the sounds of life coming from you, along with the rattle of death that appears every so often from somewhere deep inside.

I'm not sure what tomorrow will bring. I never have and never will because I have chosen to live in the moment, and one day I'll choose to die in the moment. I am here for your moment if that comes tonight. Oh, dear Mom, I will miss having you around.

You left me this message on my website Tuesday before this new phase came your way:

"I promised myself that I would love my children with every fiber of my being. I think I have accomplished that. Do they ever get tired of our hour-long good-byes, hugs over and over as the time slipped away? I think if I say it enough, it will be so! My love has no depth; it lives in an eternal cavern of joy. I can feel the love long after our good-byes. No, I will never say goodbye. Only see you on the Other Side. LVU

Like Dylan says, 'Chuckie, you are my blue-eyed son.'"

Love,
Chuck

Letter Seventeen

August 28, 2023

Dear Mom,

The watch is slicing time. There is a dancing click to the seconds, a tap dance more than a ballet, and the anticipation of when your last breath will come is agonizing. I try to remember my mindfulness and stoic studies and be completely in the moment and not focus on what is to soon come. I also attempt to remind myself that you are not mine or anyone's to keep because we are all impermanent.

I leaned over your shoulder today attempting to stand and leave, and I broke. My head fell to your body as if my core gave way at the waist and my soul collapsed. Even in your weakened state, you moved your hand from the warmth of the blankets and placed it on my head and stroked the bristles of my hair to comfort me. It proves I am still a boy, your child, and you are my mother. You will always be our mother. You proved that today as you asked both of your sons if we are taking care of ourselves and eating. There you are, dying by the moment, short of breath, pain trickling through your limbs, in a feverish state, and you are checking to see if we are okay.

When I had a moment alone with you today and we just sat holding hands, looking into one another's eyes, I said to you, "I am going to miss you. I am going to miss our talks."

"Well, we certainly have said a lot to each other in our time together, haven't we," you said. "We laid it all on the table."

"I love you," I held your hand tighter and then I had to ask a question, "I hope I was a good son?" Here I am again, seeking validation. It's something I am working on, trying to recognize that I am worthy and good enough.

"You have been a wonderful son. Ever since you were a little boy, cuddling next to my side, you have loved me and I loved you." Then, in between breaths, you said, "This is going to hurt." Once again, as always, you are trying to prepare me for tough times. It's why we are so resilient.

"I know, but it's been hurting a long time." You nodded, recognizing the pain of the past couple of years.

I cried on your shoulder some more, and you held my hand with what strength you have left, holding me a little tighter, trying to take my pain away with your touch.

Death is like a dry whisper. It is there, lingering in the air, but too shallow in its voice for us to hear quite yet. However, it is getting louder. Death is coming, and it is ready to scream. The signs of life leaving your body are all there and standing in formation like tired soldiers ready to march forward no matter the consequence of battle, and finally take over. Death will conquer. We are watching your body give itself away slowly. I wish I could put you back together and make you healthy again, but it is time. We both said it to each other today. It's time for you to leave, and we are both ready. At least, as ready as we can be. I still have this desire to just put you in my truck and drive to the woods, carrying you through the trees and letting you smell the pines again.

I am now here in your apartment, sitting among your belongings, in your chair, and I can feel your presence. I am comfortable. I am safe. I am in your home, which has always been mine. You said to me today, "When you smell chicken and dumplings, I will be there. It's me." You said the same thing to me a few days ago about walking in the woods. You told me when I see the trees sway and smell the wind, you will be next to me. I will walk the woods often and wait for those moments.

I wish you were something that death can't steal, but I am afraid it's a clever thief.

In your poem, A Fearless Death, you write, "I ask that death allow me the freedom that my life denied..." In our conversations, we have often talked about your life and its purpose, just as we have mine. In some ways, I understand why you would write that because you struggled with freedom. You became a mother at seventeen, stranded in a thoughtless marriage, raising five children, working your knuckles raw. It may seem like freedom was running from you and not attainable. Still, I always challenged your thoughts, telling you that your life has been extraordinary. I would always tell you, "We should never hope for an easy life. When we suffer, it helps us build resilience and grit, and makes us stronger. A hard life provides more stories to tell." You always liked that, and it made you feel as if you did your best. Yet, I hope that when you do pass over to wherever it is that you are going, you have the freedom and will to do what you have always dreamed of.

There's this incredible heaviness on my chest as I tell the truth I am about to share. I hope that you will pass soon. I know it is coming, but as you said, "I don't know what the good lord is waiting for. I am ready." The most loving thing that a son can want for his mother is for her to no longer suffer. Yet, it pains me to want to see you pass so you no longer have to hold the pain that you have been carrying in your body. To say that I want you to die rips out my lungs, but I know it is best for you. Because I love you, I want your death to arrive.

Oh, dear mother, it is coming soon. Death is lingering. I felt it. It is near, and it will take you from us in body, but it can never have you in mind, our mind that is. You have taken a special place in your children's thoughts, and it will stay with us until we join you.

I am not sure when these letters will stop. When will my words come to a halt? I hope that you have enjoyed them. Each word, each letter is filled with my love for you. In the sentences of each letter is my dedication to you and the life you have lived. It is your son, pouring his soul into a thought that trickles like cold water over mountain rocks in a slow-moving stream.

I keep saying I am okay. It's as if I am trying to comfort those around me that when I lose you, I will not lose myself. I am okay, but I also want to swallow the earth and then explode like a dormant volcano that came to life. I want to wreak havoc on the heavens, but I promise I will stay at least as calm as a tidal wave.

Love,
Chuck

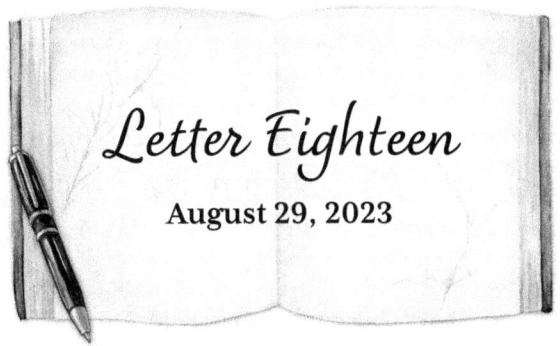

Letter Eighteen

August 29, 2023

Dear Mom,

This morning, it is silence you seek. You said that to me after we were alone. You are in need of quiet and a calm space in order to pass. "There is a white butterfly," you said as you pointed to the ceiling. Later, you paused what you were telling me and said, "There are people here; they walk in front of me one by one." You looked toward the end of the bed. "They are preparing me to go."

Anyone who has been around someone dying knows that this is natural, normal, and a sign of things to come. In my younger years, I questioned the existence of God, as a sort of rebellion, but as I grew older, and the losses started to add up, I knew there was more out there. I have seen too many things that have shown me the presence of others that are beyond our world. There is something greater than ourselves. You often told me that, but as with most things in life, we have to learn it for ourselves, often through difficult times. You said you did not recognize the people that are here for you.

"Do you feel comfortable with them?" I asked.

"Yes, they are telling me it's time. They are getting me ready."

I saw your eyes become heavy and told you it's time to rest. Rest is important while dying. You have to prepare your body for passing. I simply said, "I will read and write you another letter while you sleep. I want you to do what is needed." It was me, once again, giving you the okay to let go. "There is no more to be said or done," I added.

As I watch you sleep, I wonder how I will remember you? I mean, will it be when you were younger and I was a child? At my wedding, we danced a mother-and-son dance? Perhaps, it will be at the age I am now? My memory could hold tight to you being old, maybe even sick, because much of your old age has been weighed down with illness. I am not sure, but I predict, like all memories, that you will fade in and out of various shapes and forms and variations of who you once were. Memory is a gift, and it can be haunting.

Love,
Chuck

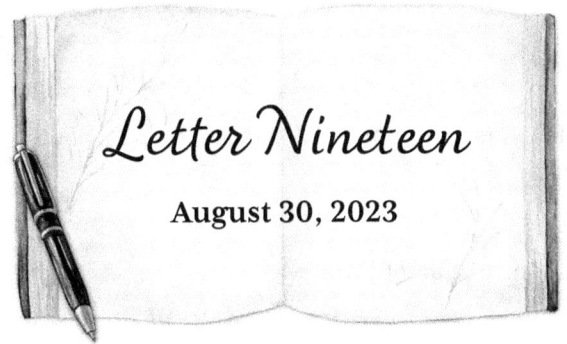

Letter Nineteen

August 30, 2023

Dear Mom,

I know who I am, so help me. For better or worse, I have always been true to myself.

I am a three-year-old boy, sitting in the grass looking up at you with a dimpled smile.

I am a five-year-old who bought you a figurine of a beautiful woman at a garage sale because I thought her dark, ceramic hair looked like yours. I still feel bad that I broke it when I was mad at you, but with my young hands, I glued it back together. Isn't that what people do when they love one another and are angry? They glue the pieces back together the best they can? Your smile and hug said you forgave me.

I am a seven-year-old who became frightened that year. The trauma started to build a solid base on my tight shoulders, and I became a kid who hid his fear so you would not know. What I knew was that your strength protected me. Your love was too strong for me to be ruined.

I am a ten-year-old with scraped knees from climbing trees. You patched me up and told me to keep climbing. I've been climbing all of my life.

I am a twelve-year-old who was losing himself in the turmoil of life. A similar chaos you recognized in yourself but didn't recognize it was getting heavy, suffocating me. You stayed loving me, never giving up, holding me accountable, and trying to show me a different way than getting placed in cuffs. You recently told that story and how you told the cops to scare the hell out of me. "Scare him straight," you said you told them. They almost did.

I am a thirteen-year-old running a touchdown with one shoe on. That story makes you laugh.

I am a fifteen-year-old who fell in love with a girl and has been ever since. Can one die of loving too much? If so, it would have happened by now.

I am a nineteen-year-old who ran the drill instructors to the ground when they challenged me in boot camp and I became a marksman in Security Police. You didn't recognize me when I returned home. Hell, I didn't recognize myself.

I am a twenty-three-year-old who said, "I do" and never looked back.

I am a twenty-five-year-old who watched my father die. I'll say it for both of us: I am glad the son of a bitch is gone and left early on. When you were hallucinating the other night, it sounds like you killed him in your sleep. That's okay. I hope it gives you closure.

I am a thirty-seven-year-old who became a teacher. It's something I never thought I would do, but tragedy pushed me towards wanting to teach. I hope I am good at it. I hope I have helped some kids along the way.

I am a forty-year-old who watched you lose a child. That is a heartbreak that cannot be sewn, not even with the strongest of stitches.

I have run obstacles all my life and made it to the end.

I have climbed mountains and fallen down a few. I have walked wooded paths that seem like they were made only for my feet, and I have seen sunsets that seemed like they were only for my eyes. I have been to Celtic nations and walked in the city lights, and I swam in oceans that spun me in the waves. Mountain lions have crossed my path on a few trail runs, and I watched black bears roam, and I talked to hundreds of young people about living their lives to the best of their ability. I have advocated for students until I was threatened by the ignorance of society, and I have written novels and was told they helped. Some said my words saved them. That is daunting to think about, but I am grateful. I have learned to forgive and I have learned to let go. I have said goodbye to friends, and I have held many a dog's paws as they passed over the rainbow. I have walked barefoot in the warm sand. I have lived a good life.

I have done a lot with the life I have had so far, but what I am most proud of is being a husband and your son. If I am good at either one of those, then I am content.

Your heart is slowing. I can feel it. My chest is heavy, and I feel like I am breathing for the both of us.

Love,
Chuck

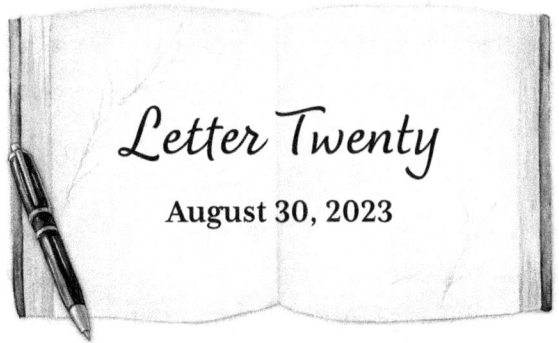

Letter Twenty

August 30, 2023

Dear Mom,

The death rattle is here with you. It has been all day. Anyone who has been around the dying knows this sound. It is haunting, uncomfortable, a drowning cadence sounds softly and continuously. I have read everything I can to prepare for this moment, and I remember my lessons from being a witness to dying in the past, so I know you are not bothered by it. It is us, the living, the ones who sit by your side, holding your hand, telling you softly, "I love you, Mom," that are shaken by the sound. I have studied death as much as I have studied life. I am a good student of both subjects.

I had a moment alone with you and told you that I was thankful you were my mother. Your eyes stayed closed but they moved underneath the lids. I told you I loved you and you gently squeezed my hand. It is evidence that you hear me. Evidence that you feel your youngest near. In fact, I know you can feel the presence of your kids in the room, even Charlotte, who passed away thirteen years ago. In fact, it is probably her that you feel nearest to, since it is Charlotte who you said you would "go home" to. She is here. There is a lot of energy in this room. The presence of those who you said were getting you prepared are here. They have been for a few days, but on this day, I can feel them close, like a feather that is stroked constantly over my skin.

You did open your eyes for a little while this evening. The words are all but gone now, but you said three words that I understood between the rattling cage that binds you, "Get me out." I did think for a moment, is this our joke about me putting you in my truck and driving west until we find mountains and dry air? Are you telling me it's time to take you far away and drive until the sun comes up? Are you indicating for me to tell you again that it's okay to let go?

My chest hurts. Oh dear mother, my chest aches and if I wasn't in good shape, if I wasn't used to the weight of grieving, I may think I was having a heart attack. Of course, being the anxiety-prone man I am, I had to look it up. The page that came up on my little wicked device told me it was "Broken Heart Syndrome." That makes sense since my heart is breaking moment by moment. So, I held your hand and meditated. I passed my energy on to you and felt yours back to me, and I summoned all of the angels from the heavens to come to you and take you away from your broken body. I am ready for them to lift you and guide you to a different light than the one we see out your window now, which is a giant moon looking down on us.

The rattle will eventually go away and then you will too. It is coming. The last breaths are close and I predict the world will shake. At the very least, it will spin a little slower and maybe off its axis. The oceans may send their waves toward the center of the Earth and crash into each other. Or, it will be nothing, except for those you created weeping over your body.

Before I take my fingers from the keys of my computer, I will tell you that you are my breath. I appreciate the life you gave me and I will use it up well. I will absorb all that life has to offer and live each day to the fullest of my abilities. I will explore and touch the trees, feeling the energy of Mother Nature, and I will sit in mountain streams and let the cold water renew my skin and heal my bones. There will be foreign lands that will hold my footprints. I will finish that novel I told you about. I will go on to celebrate the gift you gave me and I will drink the sun.

Love,

Chuck

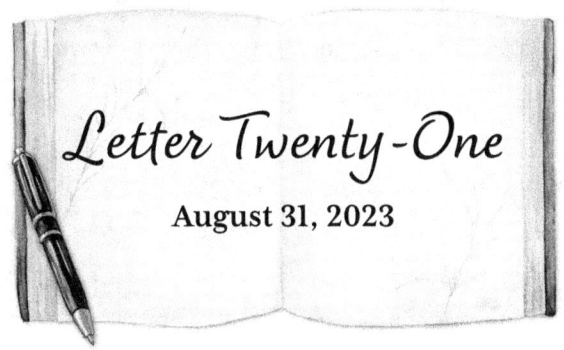

Letter Twenty-One

August 31, 2023

Dear Mom,

"Where are my babies?" You said today through a raspy, gargled throat.

"We're all okay," I said with confidence because I didn't want you to know the truth that we are cracking just a bit with each passing moment. Those moments have turned us into broken pieces trying not to fall onto the wooden floor and cause a mess.

You lay there dying, suffering, and you ask about your children. A mother is truly a protective giant. It's like you used to tell me when I was a teenager, "I can't go to sleep until I know all my children are safe."

Your dying is like an ax handle to the temple. I cannot protect you from all of this and it deflates me. I am waiting for your death to be like in the movies, something pleasant with bright light hanging over you, making your face calm, and the angels take you high in the air with an arched back and your arms fallen like wings to the side, and you have a slight smile telling us that you are going to a better place than here. Actually, sort of like Charlotte's death. However, that is not how death typically works. It's often tragic.

My brother was screaming at the gods today to let you go. If he could have, I think he would have grabbed a hammer and smashed it into the earth, cracking it in half. He would have created a worldwide earthquake. I know anger is part of grieving but our anger is because you have to suffer through this. You have had your share of suffering in your life, more than your share, and I question why sometimes. Why do you have to bear so much pain?

Dying is not always beautiful. It is harsh, painful, and leaves you drowning in your own saliva because you cannot swallow. The death rattle is fierce. The suffocating nature of the liquid and blood in your lungs is waking you up from a morphine-induced rest. You are not finding peace. Even the nurse said this morning, "We are more humane to animals than we are to people." It is true. We would never let our beloved dogs suffer this much. They would have a needle placed in their veins, and they would pass with dignity, knowing that the last act of the humans that cared for them was out of sheer and true love. How do we reconcile this?

The staff that have cared for you are wonderful. They are beautiful souls who take pride in caring for those that are passing. Yet, they are defenseless to a set of morals that was placed in an old, dusty procedural book by someone who did not want people to choose how they wanted to die and how far they wanted to take their bodies before suffering. Choice is taken from us at every stage of life, I suppose.

You awoke several times through the night and morning with pleading eyes. "Let me go," you said. Yes, dear mother, we do want to let you go and rest. The morphine is coming more often now, and you are at ease. Maybe they saw the look in our eyes that said, "This is enough."

Death alone is difficult enough to experience. Why does it have to test us with watching someone you hold so close to your heart to be trapped in misery? You did nothing to deserve this. Your life has been moral, ethical, and one that has kept love in the forefront. There are murderers that have a more peaceful death. You did warn me less than forty-eight hours ago that this was going to hurt. Damn, you were right about that! I told Karen today, "This will take a while to recover from." I was so exhausted when I said that, my head spinning in a ravaged merry-go-round, so much so that I nearly passed out. I found a cot to lay my head on and sleep for a half hour. Dying is an endurance test for us all, mostly you. When you pleaded, "Why? Let go." I held your hand and flexed the muscles that line my forearms to show you that I would remain strong. You blinked.

"I don't know how you guys are doing this?" said Karen.

"We are able to because Mom raised us to be resilient," I replied. That says a lot about you. We should all raise our children to be resilient or learn how to be for ourselves. It's the key to living a good, joyful life. However, at times, being so resilient can drain the marrow from our bones. You did well. We are drained.

I know if you were able to read this letter, Letter twenty, that you would say, "Hell, I can take it." Yes, I know you can. You have endured so much in your eighty-four years. Can you take it? Sure, but should you have to?

Your frown has settled to a pleasant sleep. I pleaded with confident eyes to the nurse to give you the maximum amount of morphine. She did. I know my request has now sent your dying into another gear, faster, with less discomfort and pain. Yes, your son has requested that you die faster, and that sacrifice is how much I love you. I told you today as we looked into one another's eyes, "It's almost over, Momma."

Love,

Chuck

Letter Twenty-Two

September 9, 2023

Dear Mom,

"This is going to hurt," you told me in our last conversation. You were preparing me for what was to come. It does! Oh, Mom, it hurts more than you know. Last conversations are often the most meaningful because of the significance of what is happening. One must hold every word that is being said and find purpose in them.

You died on a Thursday, almost midnight, and we are starting to think you predicted the date. For some reason, you kept telling Carl and me about August 31st, but with little context. It was a date you kept mentioning. Did you know?

I fell asleep next to you in the recliner, watching The Andy Griffith Show. I was in a dead sleep when I was startled and looked over at Carl and Terri staring at you and then back at me. It was distorted through Andy's voice, but I heard the words, "She stopped breathing." I attempted to stand with exhausted legs and moved quickly over your body. I couldn't cry just then. Did it happen? Were you really gone?

I was told that your breathing went from being labored and fast to normal, and then you had one large exhale, and that was it. Your breath left your lungs for the last time. Carl then said, "I have never seen anything like it, Chuck." I was still in half sleep, but I was told that right at the moment that your breathing slowed, my legs and feet started to run a "hundred miles per hour" while I slept, and when your breathing halted, so did my running, and that was when I was startled awake. What happened there? That couldn't have been a coincidence. I never run in my sleep. I know I am asking questions that will never be answered. They are questions for a dead mother who cannot respond. I have asked questions to the dead before, and sometimes, when the wind is just right through the trees, they are answered. Did you pass through me when you died?

I walked away from your body and went outside. Being outdoors, below the sky, has always given me the space to breathe. I collapsed on the patio, landed on all fours, and raised my head to the full moon and screamed like a wounded wolf. I don't remember screaming, but I was told I did. I have taken time to process this moment and I do believe my sanity left me for a moment. I was in agony, uncontrollable tension filtered through my muscles and I wanted to smash the concrete below me. I was in pain. Yes, dear mother, it hurts! Oh god, it is painful.

I took the blanket that was still around my shoulders and wrapped it tight and walked out to the grass. I remember thinking, "I need to call her. I need to hear Karen's voice to know that I am alive." I don't remember a lot of the conversation, except that I was talking slowly and deliberately, and I knew that love was on the other end. My love was still there and it gave me some clarity, so I told her I would be okay and that I loved her and then hung up.

I then sat with the blanket around my shoulders in the grass and started to breathe. I knew that in order to bring myself back from wherever it is I went, the chaos of me screaming at the moon and the moonlight screaming back, I needed to meditate. The grass was cool below and then out of the corner of my eye I saw something. I turned my head slowly and about ten yards away there was a possum. It had waddled close and then turned towards me just staring. I stared back and neither of us was startled. After a minute of looking into the possum's eyes, it went into the tall grass and disappeared. Later, when I told this story and wondered what that possum was doing there, I had to look up the spiritual significance of it. Most resources said it was, "Rebirth and reincarnation." Mom, I know you believe these things to be true. You have talked about how there is more out there than we will ever know, and we just need to pay attention. Were you reborn? Will you be a mother again like you said you would?

My grieving for you started when you told me you had Multiple Myeloma. It started a couple of years ago as we cried together as you said, "I'm not giving up. I'm going to fight this thing and stay with my children and grandchildren as long as I can." I knew what that meant. I knew that in that one single moment that you chose to suffer. You chose to show everyone what the word "grit" means. That is why you suffered during your last couple of days. You were fighting up until the end. I looked into your eyes and held them within mine for so many moments and told you, "Let go." Your son could not do anything for you, so I wanted you to know it was okay, but you wanted to fight. You have fought all of your life, so I am not sure why I'd think dying would be any different. I think if you would have submitted and passively just decided to die, that the suffering would not have happened. I believe that. I respect that. You chose to slap the shit out of death, but we cannot conquer something that we all owe.

I thought I was prepared. I did. I was naive enough to think that because I have accepted your death over two years ago, and when we sat on your patio talking about your two-month prognosis and I asked you, "Are you ready?" and you said you were and then asked me the same and I said, "I am." No one can be prepared to lose their mother. No one can be prepared to lose someone they love. However, it hurts so much because we had fifty-three years together, loving one another. The pain I am in now is worth the years we had to love each other and build our history together. The agony of losing myself to the moon that night was worth it. The pain in my chest when I entered your apartment for the first time after you died, and as the scent of your home hit my nose like a fist, which brought me to falling in your chair and weeping in pain, was all worth it. Loving someone so much that it tears you apart when you lose them is worth it.

Mom, you were never mine to keep. I know that, and I repeat it often. Hell, we talked about it. You said two Saturdays before your death, "I am eighty-four years old. I can't expect to be here with y'all forever. I couldn't bear to grow so old that I would see another one of my children die. I couldn't take that again." You're right, you couldn't take that again. I took you home after Charlotte died, and I was unsure if you would survive her loss, but you did for all of us. You gave your children all you had and then some. Still, no amount of time is enough. I want you back.

There are no more chemotherapy appointments. No more lunches on your patio. There is no more bringing you chocolate shakes and watching your eyes light up. No more helping you into my truck and hearing you try to cover up your pain with a slight moan. No more text when you wake in the morning or before you go to bed at night, just to let your sons know that you are okay. There's no more calls on the phone with your voice telling me, "Hello, hon, I love you." There are no more stories about your daddy and Uncle Curtis, and the South you grew up in. There are no more poems where you told us your truth and ours too. There is only death. It came and then left us with a silence and void that can never be filled.

I left for the north woods this week. I needed to get out into the thick of the trees and simply be. The woods have always brought me solace, and it helps me find answers and renew my soul. It's been doing that since I was little, and I am now older and wise enough to recognize that I am not whole unless I am walking or riding on a dirt path. I found some answers while I was there. Once again, I found that I am not entirely content unless my love is with me, at my side, holding my arm, and hearing her laughter. I realize that I need to return to the classroom and teach again. There are students that deserve my best, and I will try to give it to them. I also have foreign lands to wander and more trails to hike. I want to have a million more experiences and watch thousands of sunsets.

In the woods, I found a renewed desire to bring my words to the world, and I have felt like I neglected my novels in many ways.

They became less important to me the past couple of years, and so I did not bring much attention to them. In our very last conversation, you said to me, "Keep writing and bring awareness to your books. They are important. They help people. Go and speak about mental health. There are people that need to hear your story and how you have coped. Maybe you will write about me one day. Make your momma proud." That was our last full conversation we had. During your death, you turned your focus to what you wanted me to do with my life. I guess that is what a mother does. I will try, dear mother, if people are interested, I will try to bring them my words, written and spoken.

I told Karen the day after your death, "I have changed again," when I woke up sobbing into a pillow, saying, "Momma," over and over. It is true. I have said this many times over the years as I reflected on the deaths I have faced or life's challenges. We change, whether we want to or not. When we lose someone close to us, our trajectory moves in another direction. That is okay. Change is good. It is to be embraced because change helps us grow and develop. We must listen to the pain and suffering and not deny it, and then make a plan to live the life we must. I also told Karen, "I have a life to live. My mom would not want me curling up in a fetal position in a dark room, sobbing for the rest of my life." That is not who you raised. Resilience and grit, dammit, and to have the will to keep moving forward no matter what, is who you raised. I will. I will keep moving forward and make you proud, but this heaviness on my chest that is not allowing me to take a full breath will be there for a while. It is okay. I will keep breathing and release the tension that is now confining me. I will eventually have the energy to think clearly again.

It's your voice that I miss the most.

I picked your ashes up yesterday and buckled you into the front seat. I drove us to Indian Lake and stuffed you into my backpack. I know you would have laughed at the sight of me putting your remains into my blue backpack and forcing the zipper to seal you in. You said that you wish you could see the trails I love to walk on. We had a wonderful hike as the trees swayed above us and the mist fell softly through the branches. You walked beside me with nimble legs and a full heart.

This is my last letter to you. I have written you many pages of thoughts and feelings about life, death, grieving, resilience, suffering, and love. In the words, there are answers and there are questions, and with each stroke of the keys, there has been your youngest child spilling his tears and truth onto a blank page. You and I often talked about blank pages and how they offer opportunities. The white of the page can be filled with stories and it can be filled with reflections, and somewhere within the words and ideas that unfold, there is healing.

I have a blank page in front of me and a lifetime of opportunities sit before me. I must go now.

Love,

Chuck

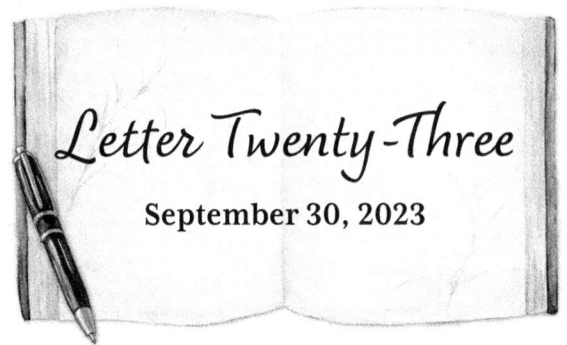

Letter Twenty-Three

September 30, 2023

Dear Mom,

It seems as if I cannot stop writing to you. Today is one month since you died. I sit and wonder some days how much sorrow I can take? I suppose I will never stop writing you letters because you will always be a part of me.

Since you left, life had to start again. I found myself in front of students about a week and a half after you died, wondering how this is possible, to simply pick up and keep going forward as if I did not experience a great loss? I do understand how life must go on and all that bullshit, but it seems like the world wants to drain me at times. I walk around faking it all day. I fake conversations and smiles, and I fake my enthusiasm to continue teaching, and I fake that I am doing okay. I have become an actor on stage from morning to night, giving my greatest performance, entertaining students and the people who surround me. I wear a mask that has a painted smile and sad eyes.

I attempted to make sense of your death and the past couple of years. I say things like, "She wasn't mine to keep," and "I am grateful for my agony because it means I was loved." I believe that with all my soul, but I am starting to wonder if I am saying it for me or the people giving their condolences? It's my attempt to help them understand grieving and loss and reframe the dialogue that surrounds death and loss. Perhaps, I am saying it for you because there is part of me relieved that you are gone, not suffering anymore? However, there is guilt that comes with that relief. I am grateful for the agony your death has produced. It is true. I miss you so much and there is a void that sits silent, making my mind pause and check reality to see if this is actually true. Did you die? I look at my phone and still see your number there, just as I still have Charlotte's. Do I call it to see if this is all a dream and you will pick up and say, "Well hey darlin, I was just thinking about you."

I push a little heart every day that carries your voice and you tell me you love me. I say each time, "I love you too, lady." Love doesn't end just because someone dies. When a bond has been established, it cannot be broken and it lasts for an eternity. I am not sure that little heart will last a lifetime. Maybe it is why I play it so often, to capture your voice in my memory, so when I am walking around with old eyes and muffled ears, I can simply breathe in deep and your voice is there. I have forgotten other voices of those that passed. I wish I had them all.

Mom, as you know, I am a reflective man, a deep thinker. Some might say, "Too deep." I sit here writing this letter to you with ghosts all around me. In front of me, there is a picture of me carrying Payton, and then Hazel and Chloe's urns. The closet to my left holds David's biking jacket and a small knife that Richard once gave me, and to my right is your curio cabinet that displays your picture, along with Charlotte and Little Daddy. Behind me, on the wood chair where I sit and write these words, is a long flannel jacket that you liked to wear on autumn days. Two of your paintings lay at my side waiting for a frame. I sometimes wonder if this room will someday be filled with more ghosts, their presence lingering over me when I write my thoughts and stories? How many others will I outlive? How much pain can one heart take?

You may wonder where Dad is? I keep his memory in a box in the basement. I don't allow him much space, physically or mentally.

I have not felt you near lately. Have you moved on to that other life you thought you would live? Have you been reborn and will you someday be a mother again? I have this recurring thought that makes me smile. One day, when I am old, will I walk into a café in some foreign land, and glance over at a younger woman holding a small child, maybe a blond-haired, dimpled boy, and he will be hanging onto his mother with all his love, and then the woman will look up at me with familiar eyes, and for a moment, just a split moment, we will have a connection telling us that we have seen one another before? We will hold our stare long enough for it to be familiar and then simply move on, and then perhaps shortly after, I will move on to my new life, leaving this one behind. Death will find me too one day.

I had someone approach me the other day. They asked me how I was doing, which I appreciated. When I am asked this, it is difficult for me to say, "Good" or "Fine." As you know, when someone asks your son a direct question, it is difficult for me not to give an honest answer. I told them that I was struggling. "Grieving is complex," I stated. "One moment you may be walking down the hall and you are calm in your mind, pleasant even, realizing again that you have a life you want to live, and then the next a thought, sound, or fragrance enters your senses, or a person comes into your view and all emotion comes spilling out of you." I was walking through Acute Care at the hospital the other day to see a student, and an old woman was in the hallway, walking with the physical therapist, shuffling along with her walker. A man behind her, obviously her son, stood tall, almost protective, behind his mother. His eyes had a familiar sadness and anticipation to them. I wanted to stop him and tell him to hang onto the moments he has left with his mother. I wanted to tell him that even though it is hard to watch her fail, it is his turn to care for her, and to learn from it all. Take in her pain. Learn what it is like to live and to die. Our mothers are our greatest teachers right up until the end. I wanted to say this to him as he passed slowly, glancing over at me. I wonder if he saw a similar tiredness in my eyes? I would tell this man, this son who now walked with a heavy chest, "You will lose her soon, and nothing, absolutely nothing, will prepare you for it. You will suffer and you may scream to the heavens while sitting in agony in the grass, losing some of your sanity and yourself. Your life is about to change, so tell her everything you need to while she is here. Tell her how much you love her and celebrate every single moment that you share a breath in the same space." Of course, I didn't tell this man anything. I moved along, faking my way to the restroom where I could have a moment to cry among the toilets. That is the reality of picking ourselves back up and moving forward.

Mom, I was fortunate to have the wisdom to tell you what I needed while you were here. I am a firm believer we must tell those we care for how we feel about them because one day we will no longer be able to. I believe it is part of the problem in society: we do not share our feelings, our emotions, and let love pass by. We keep our words trapped inside as if it is uncomfortable to tell someone how much they mean to us. To me, that is a shame, and I do not live that way. It is why I sat across from you, on the very patio furniture that I now sit on at my home, and told you, "Mom, I want you to know how thankful I am that you were my mother. I am proud to be your son, and I will miss you so much. I will miss my life with you in it. You taught me so much about how to live and helped shape me into the man I am today. I am not without flaws, but I try to live with virtue, giving to others what I can. Thank you for loving me."

Two days before you died, you said to me as I held your hand, "You have been a good son." That, dear mother, was my honor. If I can leave this world being a good son, good husband, good teacher, good human, I think I will be content.

I have never needed riches, just good conversation and love.

When I was nineteen, driving with you in the car, and we were talking about my future, I said, as many young men do, "I want to get a job and make a lot of money." I continued to talk about material things that would feed my ego. You gently said to me, and it's something I never forgot, "Hon, you were not meant for that life. You were meant to help people. I see it in you. I have seen it since you were a child. There's something different about you, and others will listen. When you live a life helping others, you don't get rich, but you get other rewards." That one conversation is why I have been serving others since that moment on. In some capacity, whether in the military, working with people with disabilities, teaching, or bringing awareness about mental health, I have lived my life to serve others, and you were right, I am not a rich man in terms of money or material things. However, I am wealthy in spirit, knowing that maybe I have helped a few people along the way. The power of one single conversation is not to be underestimated. It is why I take the time to have those conversations with young people. You have taught me to be a better teacher, a better man.

I am not sure if these letters will ever stop. There is so much more to say. Though, I look back at previous letters, the ones that you read, and I wonder for a split moment if you feel my words now. Perhaps, one day you will be that new mother with her child in a café, and when I walk in with my wrinkled face and aged hands, you will look up and see the author of the book you are holding, and its title will be Letters to My Mother.

Love,

Chuck

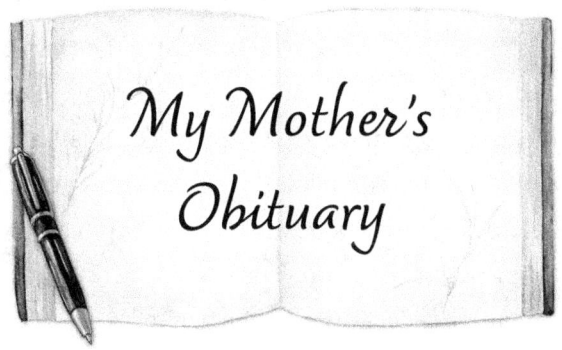

My Mother's Obituary

Some of her last words were, "Where are my babies?" Even in her last moments, Elizabeth Ann Johnson Murphree was thinking of her children. It was her purpose in life, something she often questioned, but she was meant to be a mother. In fact, in one of the last conversations she had with her son, Carl, she said, "I think I will be a mother again."

Her babies were all around her during her passing. They were all there: her daughters and sons, her grandchildren, great-grandchildren, and a great-great-grandchild. Her son-in-laws and daughter-in-laws, who she took in as her own, paid their respects and cried within her presence. At some point, she got to see them all in her last days and feel their love through their hugs and touch. It was her legacy. Everyone she created sat next to her, pleading their love until her last breaths.

Her hands were wrinkled and sometimes appeared stained by Alabama mud and hard work. She had scars that dated back to being a little girl running through the Southern countryside, scraping her knees from climbing trees, riding the wagon with her daddy, and picking cotton to help pay for food. It was the foundation of what was to come, a life of hard work, a dedication to the task at hand that surpassed most, and is often unheard of these days. She never let a lack of education stop her because it wasn't something she could control. She started raising babies at seventeen, and that doesn't allow for diplomas. Instead, she raised her children and worked her way into leading others in working jobs that were traditionally meant for men. As her oldest son said while he bent over her body, "She was an original ceiling breaker." She took pride in whatever she did and tried her best to instill those same values in her kids.

She was born a daughter to Southern parents, and the South laid a foundation in her to tell its stories that could not be told north of the Mason-Dixon line. She told them of her Uncle Curtis and how he used to throw her in the Tennessee River and yell, "Swim, hon." It was how she learned, by doing. Her eyes saddened when she talked about her Aunt Vina being like a mother to her. Oh, how she loved her. Her daddy passed away in 1977, and his death nearly ripped her soul from her spleen. For years, she welled up in tears that eventually stained her shirt when she talked about him. He was lifted up high, a man that could climb a mountain peak in a single step. She made her children believe that God had sculpted him out of stone from Cheaha Mountain. She loved to tell stories of him riding the rails and playing baseball. She loved her mother without condition and did so until the day her momma passed. Her mother taught her how to roll dumplings and that the most important ingredient when cooking was love. She loved her sisters. So much so that her eyes either changed to sadness or joy when talking about them. Billie, the oldest, was someone she looked up to. They shared a history together. And Lynn, who she often said felt like one of her own. She loved Lynn as a sister, but cherished her as if she was her own child.

She talked about how difficult her life was, but not out of pity. Instead, she tried to make sense of it. However, when asked if she had more suffering or joy in her life, she said without hesitation, "Joy! My children and grandchildren have given me so much pleasure in my life. Loving them heals any pain." That was who she was, a ferocious mother. She protected her children with all her might and allowed them to become who they would be. Her first was Patricia. She was only a teenager when Pat arrived kicking and screaming to get into this world. She used to tell her youngest, Chuck, during their conversations, "I knew when I had my first baby that I had someone to love and someone that would love me back." She created love for herself. Charlotte came shortly after. Charlotte was a magical child, her "prettiest baby" she would always say, and she was. Charlotte was a blessing to her and the entire family. Charlotte's passing in 2010 nearly took the life out of her lungs, losing a little of herself each time she mentioned her name. A parent should never have to lose a child. Terri came a few years later. She laughed when she said, "Terri came out talking and never stopped." As her third child grew to a woman, they discovered from one another that they were much alike. They had a cherished bond that represented the power of love. Her son, Carl, came five years after Terri. He was named after her father-in-law. He was her first son, sensible and smart, and she raised him to be practical and a leader, much like she was. We all take on traits from our parents. She gifted Carl her ability to lead as well as her incredible work ethic. Her last child came along a couple of years later. They named him, Charles, after his dad. She often called him her "wild boy." They had conversations that allowed both of them to dream of different worlds, and they shared a love of words.

Some of her kids had children, and when the grandkids walked into the room, it lit a fire in her eyes. They all have her blood running through them, which she took pride in. You can find features of all her relatives in each grandchild. They are her. "Their roots all run deep," she would say. She saw her granddaughters dancing at her Celebration of Life, and for a moment, she was young again with strong legs. The urge was there to stand from her wheelchair and dance with them. She had the same light in her eyes when her granddaughter leaned down to tell her goodbye one last time. She nearly lifted herself from the bed that she was confined to and hugged her with all the energy she could muster. She watched her until she walked out of the room and then laid her head back on the soft pillow, realizing it was time to start letting go. A grandson was often by her side, giving her comfort and strength. She would say to him, "You are a mix of your father and uncle," something that made her proud. She held the hands of other grandkids as they came to visit from near and far. Even though her eyes were closed forever and her breathing became labored, she knew they were there. She remembered her talks with them, and their voices brought comfort to her failing body. She knew the warmth of each of their hands and the softness in each of their voices. She loved them all. They are a part of her. She died knowing that she was loved and would be for generations to come.

She was a woman that loved animals and had many pets as a young girl, a pig being one of them. Nature and animals gave her comfort up until the day she died. All of her animal friends will meet her in heaven and walk the tall grasses by her side, except now she will have strong, mobile legs that will carry her far. Her family owes a debt of gratitude to her dog, Dixie, her main caregiver during her fight with cancer. Dixie came to her right before her diagnosis and had been a godsend ever since. A smart and witty dog, small in stature, but giant with love. Dixie's love kept her going on most days. "We don't deserve dogs," she would often say. "They are better than us."

With all that she had done as a mother, a loyal daughter, and hard worker, these weren't all that defined her. She was also a poet and a painter. She found the love of words early on as a way of expressing her pain. She would tell people, as if it were a warning, "My poems are dark." Yes, many of her poems were dark, but her words bled truth on thin paper and the blood often soaked deep enough that it healed the wounds and scars that formed on her arms and mind. She was often hesitant to share her poems and would tell her youngest about her fears. She would agree with his reply, "What do we have if we don't have our truth? Tell it the way you see it and you can't go wrong. Be honest with yourself. Be truthful in your writing." She was honest and her life's agony sang out like a Dylan song, as she bared her soul, attempting to make sense out of her eighty-four years. The words helped her pick herself up and heal the wounds that her life sliced open. It is all there in her verses, what was on her mind and the battles that she faced head-on. She left it all on the page in front of her and never compromised herself when doing so. She told her truth and hoped others would understand. If anyone wanted to truly know her, if they dared to enter her personal history without judgment, it was in her poems and her paintings.

She painted great landscapes and prairie meadows. She painted Alabama fields and the heartaches that came with working them. She painted her memory, her life on display. It started as an empty canvas that she filled up little by little, year after year. All of the joy and heartache of living a full life was placed there, for all of her children, grandchildren, great-grandchildren, and the world to see. Yes, she was a mother, but she was also an individual who absorbed life fully. She drank in all the pain and joy, the suffering and happiness, and all the love that she could.

Her last words were asking for her babies. She was a mother, not without flaws, but a damn good mother who was as strong and resilient as a mountain. Her voice is like an echo that will last a million lifetimes, and her Southern drawl will stay with all that were wise enough to listen. In her words, that dripped slowly and intentionally from her mouth, was life. The words were given to all that surrounded her. If they were good students, if they listened with both ears and absorbed her teachings, the key to surviving life is there. The lessons were taught to everyone who was in her presence and listened with intent. She wrote the book on grit and resilience. Those are two characteristics that will allow everyone to meet life's challenges head-on, smile at them, and enjoy the rest. She modeled those traits, which is what a good teacher does.

Her eighty-four years were extraordinary. They were made from love. Love she gave and love she received. We can all be so lucky to live a life like that.

Elizabeth Ann Johnson Murphree has moved on now, and with her determination, it is certain she will do what she said, "I will be a mother again."

Dear Mother, you can rest now. Charlotte is there to take you home.

Top: Growing up in Alabama
Bottom: A young mother

Top: With her daddy
Bottom: Watching football, which she loved

Near her daughter's memorial bench

One of her favorite pictures,
the summer before her passing

"The seed of suffering in you may be strong, but don't wait until you have no more suffering before allowing yourself to be happy."
- Thich Nhat Hahn